FOOD FESTIVALS

of Southern California

TRAVELER'S GUIDE AND COOKBOOK

Bob Carter

FALCON™
Helena, Montana

Published by Falcon Press® Publishing Co., Inc.
Helena and Billings, Montana

Design, typesetting, and other prepress work by Falcon Press®, Helena, Montana.

Printed in Canada.

Library of Congress Cataloging-in-Publicaion Data

Carter, Bob, 1932–
Food festivals of Southern California : traveler's guide and cookbook / Bob Carter.
p. cm.
Includes index
ISBN 1-56044-528-9 (pbk.)
1. Cookery, American—California style. 2. Festivals—California, Southern—Guidebooks. I. Title.
TX715.2.C34C3843 1997
641.59794—dc21 96-402
CIP

CONTENTS

"I like this place, and willingly would waste my time in it."
Shakespeare, *As You Like It* and motto of the Renaissance Pleasure Faire

ACKNOWLEDGMENTS

I owe my personal thanks to dozens of fellow travelers, festival organizers, residents, chefs, cooks, and food lovers for sharing their superlative recipes and treasured support with me.

Two people deserve special mention. I'm indebted to computer whiz Terry Poland for his technical advice, unlimited patience, and critical guidance throughout this endeavor. Cookbook author and food consultant Gail Hobbs made suggestions and contributed pointers that helped me immeasurably. Without their valuable contributions this book would not have been possible, nor would it have seen the light of day.

The following agencies provided a wealth of information, advice, and encouragement.

American Dairy Goat Products Association
California Apple Commission
California Avocado Commision
California Date Administrative Committee
California Dry Bean Advisory Board
California Fig Advisory Board
California Office of Tourism
California Olive Industry
California Pear Advisory Board
California Pistachio Commission
California Raisin Advisory Board
California Seafood Council
California Strawberry Advisory Board
Cherry Marketing Institute
Maine Lobster Promotion Council
Mushroom Council
National Coffee Association of U.S.A.
National Fisheries Institute
National Oyster Cook-off
Northwest Cherry Growers
Oak Glen Applegrowers Association
Sunkist Growers
U.S.A. Rice Council
Walnut Marketing Board
Wine Institute

INTRODUCTION

When I was growing up in a small California community, local celebrations were looked upon as exciting opportunities to eat sensational food, savor lively entertainment, and be as spirited as the law allowed. Californians love to have a good time. Give us an excuse, and we'll organize a noteworthy event and invite the world to attend.

Every year tens of thousands of California residents and visitors attend one or more of the state's eclectic array of food-oriented festivals and culinary celebrations. From the smallest of rural communities to the sophistication and diversity of large urban areas, hundreds of fun-for-all, hometown events take place every season of the year. California's varied festivals provide enjoyable family-style entertainment, gourmet restaurant samplings, and some of the best homemade tastes found anywhere. It's not a bad idea to plan to attend them all!

When I sat down to write this book, I had several goals in mind. I wanted to acknowledge the vital contribution California's agriculture makes to the world's food supply. I desired to highlight a wide variety of communities—large and small—and extol the diversity of their residents. Mainly, I yearned to share my overwhelming desire to experience the excitement of travel, food, and entertainment. But most of all, I hoped to inspire my readers to experience the joy of celebrating life to its fullest. I hope you'll let me know if I succeeded.

If I missed your favorite festival, or you want to contact me, I'd love to hear from you. Write me in care of *Falcon Press Publishing Company, Inc.,* P.O. Box 1718, Helena, MT 59624.

If you're so inclined, plan your traveling schedule to include one or more of my favorite events. If you do, you'll probably see me there, sampling some of the most extraordinary experiences California has to offer.

Happy trails and bon appétit!

USING THIS BOOK

For many travelers, attending a local festival or celebration helps make a trip more memorable. To avoid disappointment, it is advised you verify event dates, times, fees, and activities in advance.

Although some of the recipes have been adapted slightly for consistency in format, I've tried to allow each contributor's personality to shine through. Whenever you see a chef's hat, you'll obtain some insight into the recipe. When I've felt the need to add my bit of personal observation, you'll find it designated with a small writing pad and pen.

ORGANIZATION OF FESTIVALS: The events detailed in this book are arranged by festival name, followed by city or county location. No more than one festival in each location has been described in detail.

INFORMATION DIRECTORY: It is strongly suggested you write, call, or fax for additional information regarding destinations and events. The ***Information Directory*** portion of this guide includes contacts for individual festivals, chambers of commerce, and visitor bureaus. These agencies will provide you with details regarding accommodations, dining, shopping, recreation, attractions, and additional special events and festivals.

FURTHER FEASTINGS: Since some communities hold several food-oriented events during the year, when available these additional events have been listed in the ***Further Feastings*** section of this book.

FARMERS' MARKETS: California is well known for its agricultural variety, and many food enthusiasts visit local farmers' markets on a regular basis. This book includes a guide to local markets. You may want to visit one or more during your travels. These markets vary widely in size and offerings. If you want more specifics about each, a local telephone number is provided. Due to seasonal produce availability, it's wise to confirm dates and times in advance.

CALIFORNIA CELEBRATIONS: Each year the California Trade and Commerce Agency publishes a small booklet listing special events and ethnic celebrations for California's 12 tourism regions. A complimentary copy of the guide to nearly 1,000 reasons to celebrate may be obtained by contacting the California Division of Tourism, *California Celebrations,* P.O. Box 1499, Sacramento, CA 95812.

SPECIAL NOTE: Although diligent efforts have been made to confirm the accuracy of information contained in this work, neither the publisher nor the author is responsible for errors or inaccuracies or for changes occurring after publication. Event offerings sometimes change. To avoid disappointment, it's strongly suggested, once again, that festival date, fee, location, and specific activities be confirmed in advance.

THE FESTIVALS

1. Apple Blossom Festival, Oak Glen
2. Apple Days Festival, Julian
3. Artichoke Festival, Castroville
4. Avocado Festival, Carpinteria
5. Balloon & Wine Festival, Temecula Valley
6. Basil Festival, Paso Robles
7. Blossom Trail, Fresno County
8. Bounty of the County Food & Wine Tour, San Luis Obispo County
9. California Mid-State Beerfest, Atascadero
10. Celebration of Harvest, Santa Barbara County
11. Celebration of Herbs, Squaw Valley
12. Celebration of Western Culture, Kern County
13. Clam Festival, Pismo Beach
14. French Festival, Santa Barbara
15. Fresh Fruit Festival, Reedley
16. Grapefruit Festival, Borrego Springs
17. Grecian Festival by-the-Sea, Long Beach
18. Harbor Festival, Morro Bay
19. Harvest Festival, Arroyo Grande
20. Hollywood Bowl Summer Festival, Los Angeles/Hollywood
21. Huck Finn's Jubilee, Victorville
22. International Tamale Festival, Indio
23. Lemon Festival, Goleta

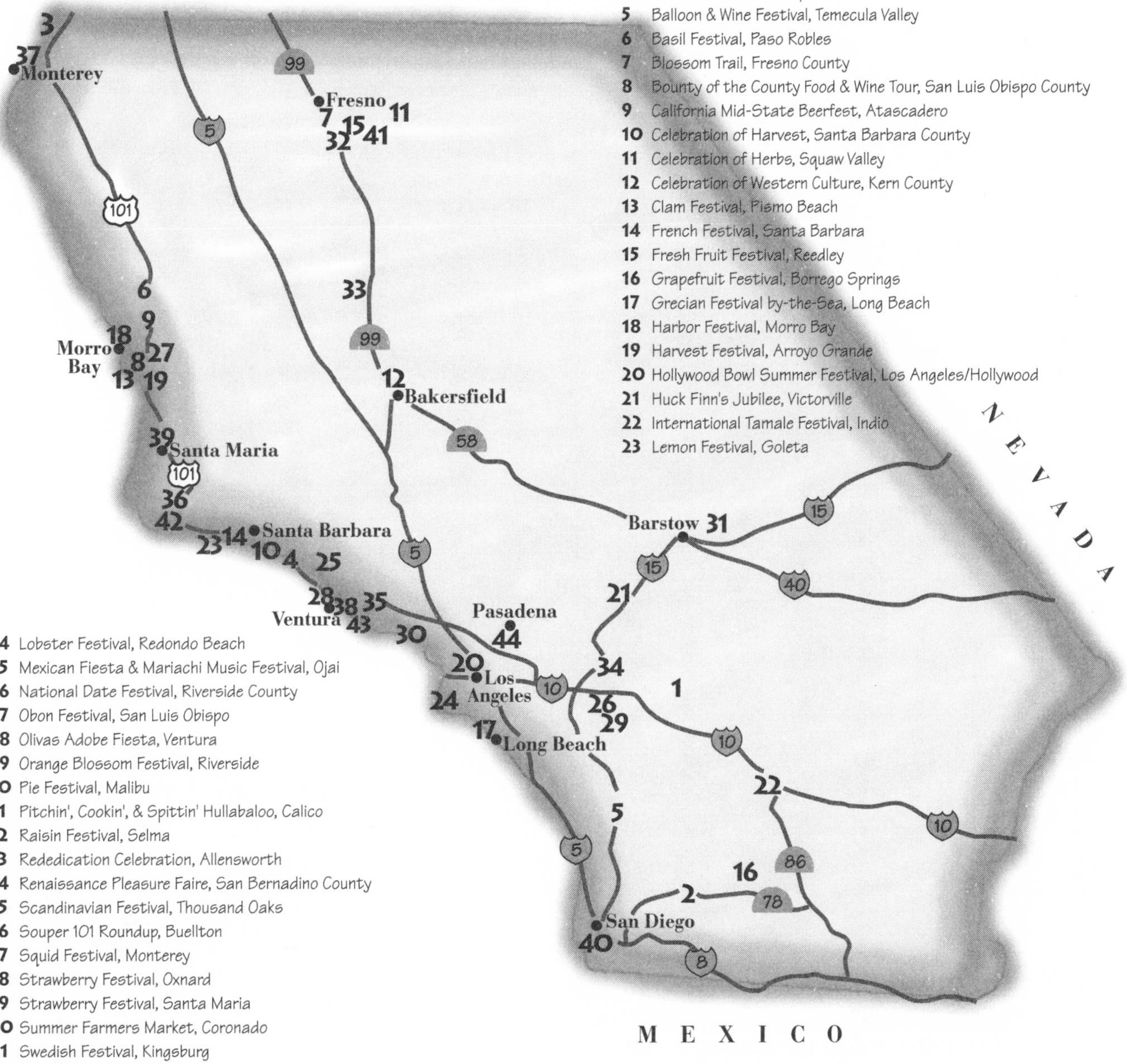

24. Lobster Festival, Redondo Beach
25. Mexican Fiesta & Mariachi Music Festival, Ojai
26. National Date Festival, Riverside County
27. Obon Festival, San Luis Obispo
28. Olivas Adobe Fiesta, Ventura
29. Orange Blossom Festival, Riverside
30. Pie Festival, Malibu
31. Pitchin', Cookin', & Spittin' Hullabaloo, Calico
32. Raisin Festival, Selma
33. Rededication Celebration, Allensworth
34. Renaissance Pleasure Faire, San Bernadino County
35. Scandinavian Festival, Thousand Oaks
36. Souper 101 Roundup, Buellton
37. Squid Festival, Monterey
38. Strawberry Festival, Oxnard
39. Strawberry Festival, Santa Maria
40. Summer Farmers Market, Coronado
41. Swedish Festival, Kingsburg
42. Taste of Solvang, Solvang
43. Taste of Ventura County, Ventura County
44. Tournament of Roses/Rose Bowl Game, Pasadena

APPLE BLOSSOM FESTIVAL

OAK GLEN

Annual. Third weekend in September.

It doesn't matter if you visit during the spring blossom season or during the celebrated apple harvest, you'll discover plenty of fun, excitement, and entertainment surrounds you in Oak Glen. The entire town dresses up during the festival. Kids are welcome to play at the small zoo or fish in the trout pond. The family will enjoy browsing for handcrafted gifts, and no one will want to miss out on the fun of filling up at the bountiful pancake breakfast.

During the Apple Blossom Festival you'll discover gift baskets filled with exceptional treats including apple butter, jams, and jellies. Seven ranches line the famous ten-mile Oak Glen Loop, where more than sixty varieties of apples are grown and picked fresh off the trees for eating, cidermaking, pie baking, cooking, and preserving. There are craft shows, wagon loads of pumpkins, apples, apple cider, and weekend pony and wagon rides.

Oak Glen's climate and the ranchers of the area blend to make this small mountain community one of the largest apple-growing regions in the southland. In the fall, at many of the ranches, you can pick your own apples and make your own cider. You can buy the apples by the bag, by the bushel, and baked in a freshly made pie right out of the oven.

To reach Oak Glen from San Bernardino, take Interstate 10 to the Beaumont exit. Go right on Beaumont Avenue, which turns into Oak Glen Road.

SPICED CIDER

2 quarts cider

$^{1}/_{4}$ cup packed brown sugar

$^{1}/_{2}$ tablespoon whole allspice

1 tablespoon whole cloves

1 cinnamon stick

$^{1}/_{4}$ teaspoon salt

dash of nutmeg

1 orange, cut in wedges

Pour apple cider into large coffee maker. Place remaining ingredients in coffee basket and brew.

Maxine Cathcart, columnist
The Valley Messenger
Yucaipa, CA

Serve this all-season drink warm or chilled.

CROCKPOT PORK ROAST WITH CIDER

Put a nice, light-colored pork roast (less expensive cuts work fine) and 2 to 3 cups fresh cider in a crockpot. Cook on low for at least 8 hours. Remove the roast, defat the remaining cooking juice, place in a saucepan, and boil rapidly until liquid is reduced by 1/2 to 2/3. Serve the sauce with the roast. Sourdough bread, steamed winter squash, and a green salad round out the meal nicely.

Annie Robertson, Manager
Los Rios Rancho
Oak Glen, CA

5 to 6 pound pork roast

2 to 3 cups fresh apple cider

WALDORF MOUSSE SALAD

1 3-ounce package lemon gelatin

1 cup boiling water

1/2 cup mayonnaise

2 cups diced apple

1 cup sliced celery

1/2 cup chopped walnuts

1/2 cup drained pineapple, cut small

1/2 cup whipping cream, whipped

red lettuce

sour cream and mayonnaise

Dissolve gelatin in boiling water. Chill until syrupy. Blend mayonnaise and gelatin until smooth, beating with mixer. Fold in apples, celery, walnuts, pineapples, and whipped cream. Turn into 1 1/2-quart mold. Chill until firm. Unmold and serve on red lettuce. Top with dressing made of half sour cream and half mayonnaise.

Maxine Cathcart, columnist
The Valley Messenger
Yucaipa, CA

OLD VIRGINIA WASSAIL

Combine ingredients and bring to a simmer. Strain and serve hot.

Annie Robertson, Manager
Los Rios Rancho
Oak Glen, CA

1/2 gallon apple cider

2 cups orange juice

1 cup lemon juice

2 cups pineapple juice

1 stick cinnamon

1 tablespoon whole cloves

sugar or honey to taste

BAKED CHICKEN WITH CIDER

1 whole chicken

2 cups fresh apple cider

1 tablespoon minced fresh garlic
(or 1 teaspoon powdered garlic)

salt, pepper, oregano, thyme,
or rosemary, if desired

1 tablespoon fresh ginger
(or 1/2 teaspoon powdered ginger)

Marinate chicken in cider overnight or for several hours. Place the marinated chicken in a shallow baking dish and sprinkle with garlic and ginger. Add salt and pepper, if desired. Crumble oregano, thyme, or rosemary over the chicken, if desired. Bake chicken in a 375° oven for 15 to 20 minutes. Baste and lower temperature to 350°. Baste often for another 30 minutes, or until chicken is done. Serve with rice.

Annie Robertson, manager
Los Rios Rancho
Oak Glen, CA

This recipe can be cooked on a stove top. Use a non-reactive pan, such as cast iron, because of the apple cider.

APPLE DAYS FESTIVAL

JULIAN

Annual. Mid-September to mid-November.

Julian's Apple Days Festival has been a tradition since 1909. You'll travel into Julian through a patchwork quilt of fall colors. The town's altitude makes it one of California's best apple-growing areas. During the harvesting period the entire community becomes a celebration. Residents and visitors combine to present fine arts shows, musical entertainment, arts and crafts, and apple-oriented seasonal activities.

Every day is apple day during the fall season in Julian. When the autumn foliage turns to red and gold, apple growing and harvesting take center stage. During the season, thousands of visitors stop at fruit stands and pick-'em-yourself ranches. If you stop and listen closely you'll hear fascinating stories about Jonathan, McIntosh, Granny Smith, and Red Bartlett. Old-time outlaws? You'll see.

Stay long enough and you'll be able to get your fill of apple pie, apple cider, apple slices, apple butter, and winter vegetables.

Not all festivals last nearly two months. However, this festival does. You might just want to hang around for it all. When you first step out of your car and smell the aroma of apple pie, or you first bite into a fresh apple or pear you've picked off the tree, you may want to stay forever.

Julian is located high in the pine- and oak-covered hills of San Diego County. This historic community was once a 1900s mining town, and today it looks much as it did then.

RICOTTA APPLESAUCE PANCAKES

1/2 cup flour

1/2 teaspoon baking powder

1/4 teaspoon salt

1/2 cup applesauce

2/3 cup lowfat ricotta cheese

2/3 cup lowfat milk

2 egg whites, beaten stiff

vegetable oil spray for pan

1 1/2 cups apple slices

vanilla lowfat yogurt

Mix flour, baking powder, and salt in a medium-size bowl. Stir in the applesauce, ricotta, and milk. Fold in stiffly beaten egg whites. Pour 1/4 of the batter on a lightly greased griddle. Tilt pan to spread batter. Cook until browned before turning. Cool.

California Apple Commission
Fresno, CA

Try layering these pancakes with apples and yogurt, then slicing into wedges and serving.

APPLE NUT MUFFINS

Heat oven to 400°. Grease 12 2x2½-inch muffin pan cups. Mix both flours, baking powder, baking soda, salt, and cinnamon in large bowl. Using electric mixer, cream butter and sugar in second bowl. Beat in eggs to blend well, then add milk. Stir wet mixture into dry mixture until just blended. Fold in apple and nuts. Spoon batter into muffin cups, filling each nearly to the top. Bake 18 to 20 minutes until lightly browned.

Walnut Marketing Board
Sacramento, CA

1¼ cups flour
½ cup wheat flour
2 teaspoons baking powder
½ teaspoon baking soda
½ teaspoon salt
½ teaspoon ground cinnamon
¼ cup butter
⅔ cup firmly packed brown sugar
2 large eggs
1 cup milk
1 large apple, peeled, cored, chopped
½ cup chopped walnuts

APPLE-WALNUT STUFFING

6 or 7 ounces dry stuffing mix

1 cup chopped walnuts

1 Granny Smith apple, chopped

4 ounces fresh mushrooms, chopped

1 cup chopped onion

2 teaspoons ground sage

2 teaspoons paprika

1 teaspoon salt

1/2 teaspoon pepper

1/2 cup melted butter mixed with
1 cup water or broth

juice of 1/2 lemon

Mix all ingredients together in a large bowl. Brush an 8-inch baking dish with melted butter and fill with stuffing. Cover and bake in a 350° oven for 25 minutes, then uncover and bake for 10 minutes more.

Gail Hobbs
Cookbook author and food journalist
Ventura, CA

This savory stuffing may be baked alone or used to stuff a 7 or 8 pound turkey. It can be doubled to accommodate a large bird. Freezes well.

MY MOTHER'S APPLE PIE

Double Crust

$1\frac{1}{2}$ cups flour

$\frac{1}{2}$ teaspoon salt

$\frac{2}{3}$ rounded cup Crisco

3 tablespoons plus
1 teaspoon ice cold water

6 cups sliced tart apples

$\frac{1}{2}$ to $\frac{3}{4}$ cup sugar

$\frac{3}{4}$ teaspoon cinnamon

1 teaspoon butter

With pastry blender, blend flour and salt with Crisco until nice and crumbly. Add water. Use flour on hands to mold into a ball. Spread out a pastry cloth covered in flour. Cover the rolling pin with a rolling pin sock and work flour into it as well. Use $\frac{1}{2}$ of the ball plus a little extra for bottom crust, roll out and gently fit it with your hands to all the bottom and side surfaces of the pan. Roll the top crust to correct size.

Heat oven to 425°. Heap thinly sliced apples in pastry-lined pie pan. Sprinkle sugar over slices of apples. Add cinnamon, dot with butter, cover with top crust, seal, and flute. Make knife cuts for air holes and bake 50 to 60 minutes. Stick a long-pronged fork in the pie to test for doneness.

Mary Clark
Calabasas, CA

"My mom sent it to me in 1956 . . . the secret to the pie crust is not using too much water. I always put exactly 10 teaspoons of ice cold water in a double pie crust."

ARTICHOKE FESTIVAL

CASTROVILLE

Annual. September weekend varies.

The Castroville Artichoke Festival honors both the town of Castroville and the vegetable that is its primary claim to fame. One of California's oldest agricultural festivals, it's moving toward its Golden Anniversary.

During this first-rate celebration, you'll discover how to trim, boil, steam, bake, fry, sauté, microwave, and just plain cook this thrilling thistle. Demonstrations and sample tastings are held hourly during the weekend. The Artichoke Festival Recipe Contest is open to amateur cooks. Fresh artichokes must be used in recipes for appetizers, soups, salads, or entrées. Entrants from all over California take part and compete for prizes.

The Artichoke Eating Contest is so unusual it has been featured in *Time* magazine, and on television's *America's Funniest People* and on *Good Morning America*. Contestants are chosen from the audience to participate in this no-etiquette contest.

The schedule of events includes several stages with lively entertainment and a parade featuring floats, horses, bands, and a host of fun-loving participants. Throughout the weekend, you'll find artichoke-growing demonstrations, a run/walk race, artichoke cooking, food specialty booths, tastings, and free recipes. For youngsters, Kiddie Korner is filled with exciting pony rides, clowns, game booths, a bounce-about, and special entertainment designed for kids.

MARINATED ARTICHOKES

Bring water, white vinegar, garlic, and salt to a rolling boil. Stir in artichokes. Continue stirring for 1 minute. Cover and boil for 12 to 15 minutes or until tender. Drain and let cool. Cut artichokes into halves or quarters, depending on size. (If there are any purple leaves, snip off.) Mix together wine vinegar, oil, garlic powder, and parsley. Add artichokes. Stir, cover, and refrigerate.

Castroville Artichoke Festival
Castroville, CA

Fresh California artichokes are available in most markets throughout the year. These marinated artichokes are better on the second day. They'll keep several weeks in the refrigerator, if stirred occasionally.

- 3 quarts water
- 2 cups white vinegar
- 3 cloves garlic
- 1 teaspoon salt
- 24 baby artichokes, whole but trimmed to edible stage
- 1 cup wine vinegar
- 1 cup salad or olive oil
- ½ teaspoon garlic powder
- 3 tablespoons minced parsley

ARTICHOKE TOSTADA PLATTER

1 pound ground beef

1/2 cup chopped onion

1 clove garlic, minced

1 cup drained kidney beans

cooking oil

6 10-inch flour tortillas

1 cup Cara Mia Picante Artichoke Hearts, cut into bite-size pieces

1 small head iceberg lettuce, shredded

1 cup shredded American cheese (4 ounces)

creamy Italian salad dressing

Sauté beef, onion, and garlic in large skillet until meat is brown. Drain off fat. Mix in kidney beans, heat, set aside, and keep warm. In another skillet, heat about 1/4-inch cooking oil and dip tortilla in one at a time. Fry about 30 seconds on each side until golden and drain on paper towels. Place each tortilla in center of a dinner plate and divide ingredients in layers evenly as follows: bottom layer spread with meat-bean combination, followed by artichokes with sauce, lettuce, cheese, and drizzle with salad dressing.

Castroville Artichoke Festival
Castroville, CA

ARTICHOKE PASTA SALAD

In a large mixing bowl, mix artichoke hearts, cut into bite size pieces, with sour cream. Set aside. Cook pasta according to package directions and chill. Combine artichoke and sour cream mixture with pasta. Chill until thoroughly cold. Taste and season with salt and pepper or seasoned salt. Serve on a bed of lettuce, and for color contrast, garnish with sprig of parsley, watercress, or sliced green onions with tops.

Castroville Artichoke Festival
Castroville, CA

1 14¾-ounce jar Cara Mia Picante Artichoke Hearts

½ cup sour cream

1-pound package fusilli or other corkscrew-shaped pasta

salt and pepper or seasoned salt to taste

lettuce leaves, parsley, watercress, or green onion for garnish

ARTICHOKE DIP

1 14-ounce jar unmarinated artichoke hearts

1 cup mayonnaise

3/4 cup shredded or grated Parmesan cheese

1 4-ounce can Ortega chiles, chopped

Cut hearts into quarters, mix well with other ingredients. Bake in 350° oven for 35 minutes. Serve warm with party crackers.

Barbara Weber
Oak View, CA

Whenever I visit my friend Barbara Weber, I ask her to put this tasty dip on her menu. It's the perfect beginning to any feasting.

AVOCADO FESTIVAL

CARPINTERIA

Annual. First weekend in October.

Nearly half the avocados grown in the United States are raised in California's Carpinteria Valley. It's logical that this local agricultural product would warrant a tasty and entertaining annual celebration to honor the versatility of this interesting fruit.

The fruit's ripe for picking at dozens of festival booths where cooks and chefs offer a bountiful array of international foods. Festival favorites include avocado-embellished ice cream, Mexican specialties, Japanese sushi, chocolate brownies, shrimp cocktails, pizza, and tri-tip sandwiches. The popular Guacamole Alley is filled with things to buy, including avocados, avocado products, cookbooks, and seedlings.

A highlight of each year's event is the world's largest bowl of guacamole. It contains more than 200 gallons of dip and serves more than 12,000 festival goers. Once you've tried the dip, head to the main stage area and take part in the Avocado Cream Pie-eating Contest.

If you want to work off some of the food tastings, consider joining the Big Avocado Run on Sunday. All you need to do is register the morning of the event and join hundreds of others as they run, walk, and stroll along the scenic course. Sports enthusiasts are welcome at several weekend competitions including the Avocado Softball Tournament and the Avocado Golf Tournament.

(Continued)

In addition to food, you'll find plenty of goodies to purchase and take home with you. Vendors sell items that include everything from exquisite carvings made from avocado pits to brightly painted wooden toys from avocado wood.

Musical entertainment and performances by magicians, jugglers, dancers, puppeteers, and mimes occur throughout the festival site, on the Guacamole Bowl stage, and at the kids' Avocado Land. Hey, you can even enjoy a program of some of California's very best "Guac'n'roll." Other features greening up the festival are colorful and eclectic arts and crafts, a flower and plant show, and a fresh produce farmers' market.

To get to the festival from U.S. Highway 101, exit at Casitas Pass road and follow the signs to convenient parking areas and shuttle buses. (Carpinteria is located between Ventura and Santa Barbara off Highway 101.)

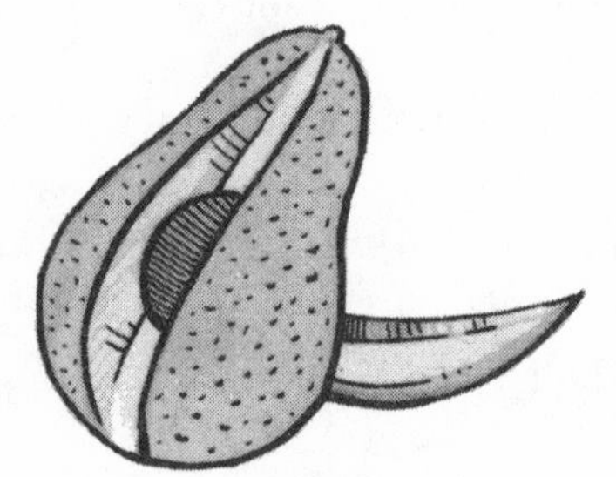

AVOCADO SORBET

Bring sugar, corn syrup, and water to boil in large saucepan. Remove from heat and stir in grated lime peel. Cool 1 hour. Blend avocados and lemon and lime juice in blender or food processor until smooth. Add cooked sugar mixture and blend until thoroughly combined. Pour into 13x9x2-inch pan. Freeze 1 hour. Remove sorbet from freezer and beat 2 to 3 minutes until light and creamy. Pour back into pan, cover with plastic wrap, and freeze until firm, about 4 hours. Makes 1 quart. Serve with fresh raspberries and crisp cookies.

California Avocado Festival
Carpinteria, CA

1 cup sugar

1 cup light corn syrup

2 cups water

1 teaspoon grated lime peel

3 avocados, seeded, peeled, and mashed

2 tablespoons lemon juice

1 tablespoon lime juice

fresh raspberries and crisp cookies

CARPINTERIA PARTY DIP

1 16-ounce can refried beans

1 4-ounce can green chilies, chopped

1 envelope taco seasoning mix

2 ripe avocados, seeded and peeled

1 tablespoon lemon juice

taco sauce to taste

shredded lettuce

1 tomato, chopped

sliced ripe olives

shredded cheddar cheese

1 cup sour cream

tortilla chips

In a small bowl, mix together refried beans, chilies, and taco seasoning mix. Spread over serving platter. Coarsely mash together avocados, lemon juice, and taco sauce and spread over bean mixture. Top with lettuce, tomato, olive, cheese, and sour cream. Serve with tortilla chips.

California Avocado Festival
Carpinteria, CA

WORLD'S BIGGEST VAT OF GUACAMOLE

With the help of cheerleaders and a football team, chop and mash all ingredients. Be prepared to engage in "GO, GUAC, GO" cheers. Allow 4 to 6 hours for preparation. Be sure to have at least 20 boxes of tissue on hand for the onion chopping.

Mix well with a boat oar in a good-size wading pool. Somehow, keep the mixture well chilled. Serve with tons of crispy tortilla chips. Makes about 12,000 servings.

California Avocado Festival
Carpinteria, CA

This is the recipe featured at the California Avocado Festival.

- 2,000 ripe avocadoes
- 2,650 chilies
- 700 garlic cloves
- 700 tomatoes
- 330 onions
- 40 pounds grated jack cheese
- 40 cups cilantro
- juice of 80 lemons
- $3^2/_3$ cups salt
- 9 cups pepper

STEAK FAJITAS

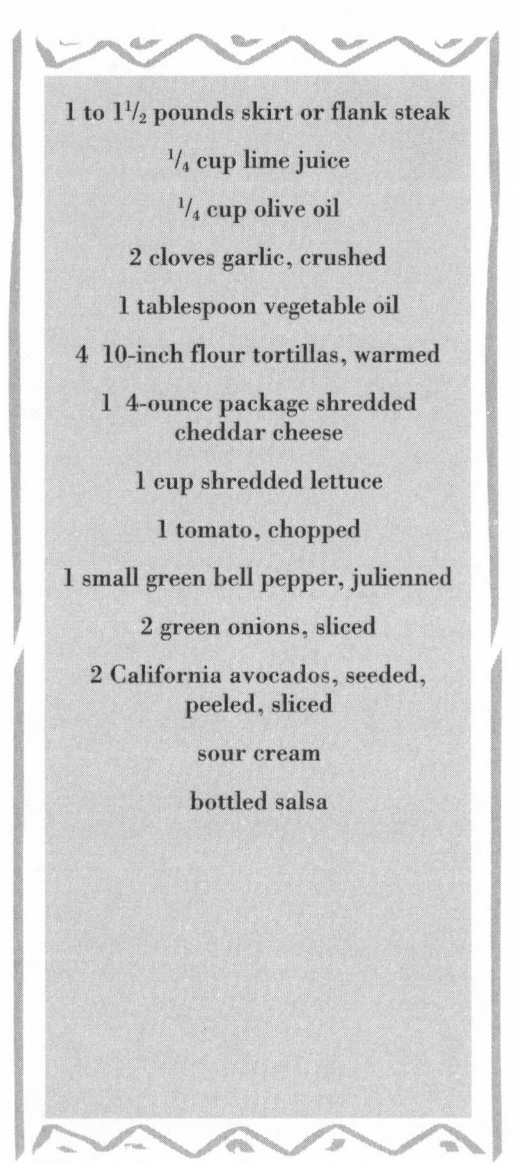

1 to $1^1/_2$ pounds skirt or flank steak

$^1/_4$ cup lime juice

$^1/_4$ cup olive oil

2 cloves garlic, crushed

1 tablespoon vegetable oil

4 10-inch flour tortillas, warmed

1 4-ounce package shredded cheddar cheese

1 cup shredded lettuce

1 tomato, chopped

1 small green bell pepper, julienned

2 green onions, sliced

2 California avocados, seeded, peeled, sliced

sour cream

bottled salsa

Slice steak into $^1/_2$-inch strips. Mix lime juice, olive oil, and garlic in medium bowl. Add meat and refrigerate at least 1 hour or overnight. Heat oil in heavy skillet, fry meat quickly over medium-high heat until browned, then remove from heat. Fill each warm tortilla with about $^3/_4$ cup meat. Divide cheese, lettuce, tomato, green pepper, green onions, and avocado slices among tortillas. Serve with sour cream and salsa.

California Avocado Commission
Santa Ana, CA

BALLOON & WINE FESTIVAL

TEMECULA VALLEY

Annual. April weekend varies.

Is there anything more spectacular than witnessing the explosion of color in the early morning sky as dozens of hot-air balloons make their ascension? I think not.

A tradition since 1983, the Temecula Valley Balloon & Wine Festival is one of the West Coast's premier family events. The enchantment begins on Friday evening with the iridescent spectacle known as Balloon Glow. During the glow, tethered balloons remain grounded while the pilots simultaneously ignite their burners, forming an illumination of brilliant colors. Temecula's balloon glow is synchronized to a selection of music.

Early Saturday and Sunday, more than fifty rainbow-colored balloons are launched from the festival grounds. They return to the festival grounds in the evening. The weekend celebration includes two evening glows on Friday and Saturday. Saturday and Sunday offer wine tasting, top headline entertainment, and a variety of family entertainment. The Kids' Faire includes a circus, bike and blade show, stage entertainment, strolling clowns, entertainers, and a petting zoo.

During the weekend, beverage suppliers provide sipping samples. Wine lovers have the opportunity to talk with vintners while tasting the premium wines from local wineries. There's gourmet cheese tasting, too, and plenty of exciting entertainment on the International Jazz Stage.

(Continued)

Located 90 miles southeast of Los Angeles and 60 miles north of San Diego is Temecula Valley, a Southern California destination worth experiencing and exploring. Over the centuries, well-known men and women have enjoyed the valley's charm. Among them are Shoshone Indians, U.S. frontiersman Kit Carson, authors Erle Stanley Gardner and Helen Hunt Jackson, and American trader and explorer Jedediah Smith.

The event is held at Lake Skinner County Park, which includes a 1,200-acre reservoir and the 10,000-acre Southwest Riverside County Multi-Species Reserve.

BOSC PEARS POACHED IN THORNTON PINOT NOIR

Combine all ingredients in a wide pot. Simmer pears until fork tender (about 1 to $1^1/_2$ hours). Remove pears to cool. Reduce poaching liquid to 1 cup (liquid will become thick and syrupy.) To serve, ladle a small amount of pear liquid onto 6 plates. Place pears atop sauce. Garnish with whipped cream and fresh berries.

Executive Chef Steve Pickell
Cafe Champagne
Temecula, CA

6 firm Bosc pears, peeled and core removed, bottom sliced off (to allow pear to stand upright)

1 bottle Thornton Pinot Noir

1 cup sugar

1 cinnamon stick

2 whole cloves

$2^1/_2$ cups water

juice of 1 lemon

whipped cream

fresh berries for garnish

SEAFOOD CIOPPINO

Cioppino Sauce

1 tablespoon minced garlic

1 tablespoon minced shallots

1/2 tablespoon minced ginger

2 tablespoons olive oil

1 bay leaf

1 tablespoon minced fresh basil

1 tablespoon minced fresh cilantro

1 teaspoon dried oregano

1/2 teaspoon salt

1/2 teaspoon sugar

2 cups Culbertson Brut

1 14-ounce can diced tomato

8 ounces clam juice

Fish & Shellfish

2 ounces olive oil

12 16/20-count shrimp, peeled and deveined

8 ounces sea scallops

8 ounces salmon, diced

12 fresh Manilla clams

8 ounces cooked Dungeness crabmeat

8 ounces cooked lobster meat, diced

Sauté garlic, shallots, and ginger in the olive oil until soft (about 2 minutes). Add everything else except champagne, tomatoes, and clam juice. Stir together until mixed thoroughly (about 1 minute). Add champagne, tomatoes, and clam juice, and simmer 1 hour to develop flavors.

In a large pot, add 2 ounces of olive oil and heat over high flame. Add all fish except crab and lobster. Sauté 1 to 2 minutes. Add the cioppino sauce, simmer until clams open (4 to 5 minutes). Add crab and lobster to sauce, and serve.

Executive Chef Steve Pickell
Cafe Champagne
Temecula, CA

ROASTED CORN CILANTRO SOUP

3 ounces olive oil

2 large onions, chopped

2 cloves garlic, crushed

3 stalks of celery, chopped

salt and pepper to taste

15 to 20 large ears of corn, roasted and cut

3/4 gallon chicken stock

3 bunches cilantro

3 large tomatoes, diced

1 chipotle, diced

In a large pot, heat the olive oil and add onions, garlic, celery, salt, and pepper. Cook until tender, about 8 minutes. Add roasted corn and chicken stock. Simmer 30 minutes. Then bring to a boil, remove from heat, and add 2 bunches of cilantro. Purée the mixture until desired texture is reached. If a completely smooth texture is desired, force through a sieve. Bring soup back to a simmer and taste for seasoning. Add tomatoes and remaining chipotle; garnish with rest of cilantro.

Temecula Creek Inn
Temecula, CA

BASIL FESTIVAL

Paso Robles

Annual. First Saturday in August.

6

Sycamore Farms is a wonderful place to visit, no matter what season you happen to be in Paso Robles. However, if you can visit only one time each year, you'll want to choose the first Saturday in August so you can take in the farm's annual Basil Festival. Here is a festival where basil reigns supreme. Sycamore Farms makes it their mission to do for basil what Gilroy did for garlic.

In a phenomenal area of rich soil, golden fields, and rolling hills, you'll discover a cornucopia of tasty delights and delectable herbs. Besides plenty of live entertainment, you'll find basil workshops, basil recipes, wine tasting, and basil-oriented food, plus beverages for sale. For the kids there are balloons, geese, ducks, chickens, and lambs located around the festival area.

Wine novices and aficionados will discover the Paso Robles area contains more than twenty-five wineries and one hundred vineyards growing premium wine grapes. You may want to schedule time to visit several during your stay. Many of the wineries provide tastings, tours, and picnic areas.

Although specialties change each year, recent festivals have included basil-vanilla ice cream, basil-infused olive oils, basil-flavored popcorn, and basil-flavored jellies and mustards.

Sycamore Farms and the Basil Festival are located 3 miles west of U.S. Highway 101 on California Highway 46 in Paso Robles.

PATTI'S PESTO BUTTER

4 cups fresh sweet basil

3 tablespoons olive oil

1 bulb of garlic, separated and peeled

1 pound butter (must be butter), room temperature

$1^1/_2$ cups pine nuts

1 cup freshly grated Parmesan cheese

Place fresh basil in a food processor fitted with a steel blade. Turn on and add oil in steady stream through feed tube. Add half of the garlic and butter and process until smooth. Add remaining garlic and butter and continue to blend. Add pine nuts and cheese and blend until smooth. This butter refrigerates well for up to 3 months, but it will never last that long. Great on toasted English muffins, baked potatoes, and steamed vegetables, and as a flavor treat in omelets.

Patricia Ballard, author
Fine Wine in Food and Wine in Everyday Cooking
Paso Robles, CA

GARLIC TOAST WITH SWEET AND SOUR GREEN SAUCE

3 tablespoons finely chopped, fresh basil

3 tablespoons finely chopped, fresh thyme

4 tablespoons chopped fresh parsley

3 teaspoons fresh mint

1/3 cup olive oil

3 tablespoons red wine vinegar

1 tablespoon sugar

2 cloves garlic, crushed

salt and pepper

1 baguette, sliced into 12 pieces

Combine all the ingredients. Mix well and let sit 30 minutes. Spread on warm toasted baguette rounds and serve.

Nancy Hayward
Basil Festival
Paso Robles, CA

PENNE WITH FRESH BASIL AND TOMATOES

Begin preparing while your pasta water heats. Uniformly chop the fresh mozzarella and tomatoes into 1/2-inch cubes. Crush the garlic, and have your olive oil ready. Coarsely chop the basil leaves right before the pasta is cooked al dente. Strain the pasta and return it to the cooking pot. Add mozzarella, garlic, and olive oil; then add basil, tomatoes, and salt and pepper. The cheese should be melting as you gently stir.

Laura Randolf
Basil Festival
Paso Robles, CA

1 10- to 16-ounce ball fresh mozzarella

2 large tomatoes

1 or 2 cloves garlic

1 cup fresh basil

1 14-ounce package penne rigate pasta

1/2 cup extra virgin olive oil (or less)

salt and pepper to taste

BLOSSOM TRAIL

FRESNO COUNTY

Annual. Mid-February to mid-March.

7

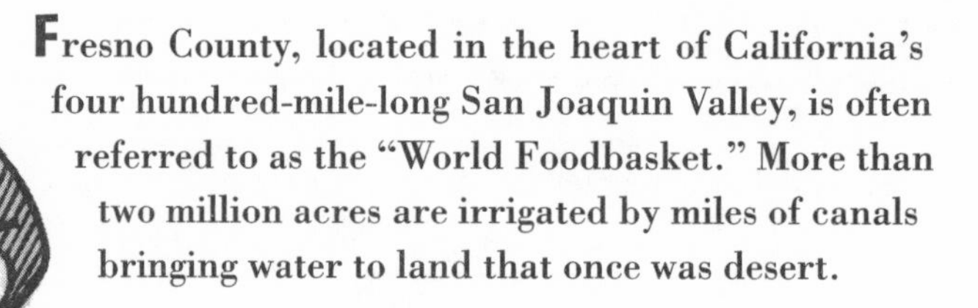

Fresno County, located in the heart of California's four hundred-mile-long San Joaquin Valley, is often referred to as the "World Foodbasket." More than two million acres are irrigated by miles of canals bringing water to land that once was desert.

Spring is a delightful reason and season to travel Fresno County's seasonal Blossom Trail and explore the beauty of California agriculture and some historic points along the way.

Whether you're interested in fresh baked pastry, photography, agriculture, botany, history, or just the great outdoors, the sixty-three-mile self-guided driving tour takes you through the spectacular blossoms of the season.

Blossoms in hues to suit every fancy include peach, plum, nectarine, and almond. There are plenty of stops along the way where you can savor the results of the spectacular blossoms. Stop and try peach pie, plum and nectarine jams, oranges, lemons, and other delectable food delights.

Wildflowers are profuse along the Blossom Trail. Some of the most commonly seen are lupine, poppies, asters, and wild mustard. The flowers complement the color and beauty of the tree blossoms along the trail. Several picnic areas can be found in Reedley and Sanger.

A free Blossom Trail map, with directions and list of attractions, is available from the Fresno/Fresno County Convention & Visitors Bureau.

APRICOT BREAD

In small saucepan on medium heat, combine apricot nectar, raisins, and apricots and cook 5 minutes. Put remaining ingredients in mixer bowl. Add apricot mixture. Mix at medium speed for 3 minutes. Pour into 2 prepared 8x4-inch loaf pans. Bake for 50 to 60 minutes at 350°.

Lee Potts
Blossom Trail tour guide
Fresno, CA

1 12-ounce can apricot nectar

1½ cups raisins

1 cup chopped dried apricots

1½ cups chopped walnuts

1 tablespoon grated orange peel

2 tablespoons shortening

2 teaspoons baking soda

2¼ cups flour

1 cup sugar

⅓ cup milk

1 egg

1 teaspoon salt

EASY RAISIN BUTTERSCOTCH PIE

Crust

1 1/3 cups sifted flour

1/2 teaspoon salt

1/2 cup shortening

3 tablespoons cold water

Filling

1 3.4-ounce package vanilla instant pudding

1 3.4-ounce package butterscotch instant pudding

2 cups milk

16 ounces sour cream

1 cup raisins, plumped and drained

1 banana

whipped cream or whipped topping

Combine flour, salt, and shortening into coarse crumbs. Sprinkle with water and toss with fork. Work dough into a firm ball with your hands. Shape into a ball. Roll out on a lightly floured board to make a large 9-inch crust. Lay into a pie pan, flute edges, prick bottom and sides thoroughly with fork. Bake at 425°for 10 to 12 minutes or until nicely brown. Cool.

Beat puddings with milk until thick and fold in sour cream. Add raisins. Slice banana over bottom of baked and cooled pie shell. Pour pudding mixture over banana. Refrigerate.

Bob Magnuson
Blossom Trail tour guide
Fresno, CA

MICROWAVE BLOSSOM TRAIL JAM

2 cups strawberries, apricots, peaches, plums, or a combination of any two fruits, coarsely chopped.

1/4 cup sugar

1 teaspoon lemon juice

Place fruit, sugar, and lemon juice in a 6-cup non-metal bowl. Cook uncovered in a microwave oven on full power until fruit mixture is thick enough to be spreadable, about 16 minutes. Stir after first 8 minutes. Jam will thicken slightly as it cools. Store in refrigerator.

Beth Richardson
Blossom Trail tour guide
Fresno, CA

FRESH PEAR PIE

pastry for a 9-inch, 2-crust pie

1/2 cup sugar

1 tablespoon tapioca
(or 3 tablespoons flour)

1/8 teaspoon nutmeg

4 cups pared, sliced pears
(about 7 medium)

1 tablespoon lemon juice

2 tablespoons butter

Mix all ingredients and pour into pastry-lined pie pan. Top with butter. Cover with top crust. Flute edges and slit top. Cover edge with foil to prevent excessive browning. Bake at 425° for 40 to 50 minutes or until juice starts to bubble. Remove foil last 15 minutes.

Mary Burnett
Blossom Trail tour guide
Fresno, CA

BOUNTY OF THE COUNTY FOOD & WINE TOUR

SAN LUIS OBISPO COUNTY

Year-round.

8

Whenever you visit San Luis Obispo County, it's the right time to celebrate the Bounty of the County Food and Wine Tour, a year-round celebration of food and wine. By taking one of four self-guided tours, you can sample a selection of gourmet foods and beverages. For example, you can taste cookies and muffins made from scratch, and sample seasonal beers brewed with all-natural ingredients. Or perhaps you'd prefer some freshly roasted coffee to go along with hot-from-the-oven pies.

In order to thoroughly experience the entire bounty, you may want to plan several visits. That way you can devote an appropriate amount of time to enjoying the bountiful selection of locally made food and wine products.

From sandy dunes to rocky shores, the 80-mile corridor between Pismo Beach and San Simeon in San Luis Obispo County is home to some of the world's most spectacular beaches and picture-postcard communities along California's central coast.

You can pick up a free Bounty of the County tour guide at the San Luis Obisbo Visitor Center. The guide's filled with suggested itineraries, delicious descriptions of tempting treats, and suggestions for eating locations along the route.

EASY ORANGE FRENCH TOAST

$^1/_2$ cup orange juice

$^1/_4$ cup low fat milk

1 tablespoon grated orange peel

4 eggs

$^1/_2$ teaspoon vanilla

$^1/_3$ cup sugar

$^1/_4$ teaspoon nutmeg

8 slices day-old bread

Mix all ingredients except bread. Place 8 slices, day-old San Luis Sourdough Wheat Raisin Bread in single layer in 13x9x2-inch pan. Pour egg mixture over bread, let soak, turning once until most of the fluid is absorbed, about 5 minutes. Place soaked slices in single layer on well-greased baking sheet and bake at 375° about 20 minutes.

San Luis Sourdough
San Luis Obispo, CA

The San Luis Sourdough bread is the secret ingredient that makes this wake-up call special.

BLACK BEAN SOUP

1 pound black beans

1 onion, chopped

1 carrot, chopped

1 stalk celery, chopped

6 cloves garlic, minced

1 ham bone or 1 cup ham skin/scraps

2 to 3 quarts chicken stock

$1\frac{1}{2}$ tablespoons ground cumin

2 tablespoons chili powder

$\frac{1}{2}$ cup sour cream

2 tablespoons milk

salt to taste

$\frac{1}{2}$ cup fresh tomato salsa

Rinse and sort beans. Put beans, onion, carrot, celery, garlic, ham bone, and chicken stock to cover in a heavy pot. Bring to a boil and skim off any froth that rises. Simmer slowly, loosely covered, until the beans are tender, about 2 hours. Add more stock if the level falls below the surface of the beans and stir often to prevent sticking. When the beans are cooked, purée them in a food processor, adding the cumin and chili powder. Mix the sour cream and milk until smooth. Heat the bean purée, adding more stock to get a consistency that will pour out of a ladle like thin hot cereal. Season with salt and pour into warm soup bowls. Drizzle sour cream over each serving and put salsa in the center.

The Wild Horse Winery & Vineyards
Templeton, CA

Serve with warm corn bread, a tossed salad, and Merlot, Pinot Noir, or Cabernet Sauvignon.

COOL COFFEES

Iced Coffee Tropical

chopped ice

$^2/_3$ cup double-strength, slow-roasted cold coffee

1 tablespoon sugar

Snow-Capped Mocha

$^3/_4$ cup slow roasted coffee, $1^1/_2$ times usual strength

2 tablespoons chocolate syrup

cream

whipped cream

ICED COFFEE TROPICAL

Fill electric blender half full of finely chopped ice. Add $^2/_3$ cup double-strength SLO (San Luis Obispo) roasted cold coffee and 1 rounded tablespoon of very finely granulated sugar. Blend until thick and creamy. Serve at once, makes two servings.

SNOW-CAPPED MOCHA

For each serving, combine $^3/_4$ cup of hot SLO roasted coffee (brewed about $1^1/_2$ times as strong as usual) with 2 tablespoons chocolate syrup and blend well. Pour over ice cubes in tall glasses and add cream to taste. Top with generous fluffs of whipped cream and serve immediately.

Central Coast Coffee Roasting Company
Los Osos, CA

San Luis Obispo is SLO. You'll see SLO (pronounced "slow") all over town. There are SLO curves ahead, SLO ice cream, SLO lanes, and, yes, even SLO plumbing. You get the idea. The abbreviation is used often, and you'll hear it from natives and visitors alike.

SAUTÉED MUSHROOM APPETIZER

Melt 1/2 tablespoon butter and add to olive oil in pan. Add mushrooms, sauté until just tender. Add beef stock and seasoning, simmer until done. Remove mushrooms and keep warm. Increase heat and reduce stock to 1/4 cup, swirl in remaining butter. Add mushrooms to sauce and serve over individual slices of toast, salt and pepper to taste. Sprinkle goat cheese over top and allow to melt slightly and serve.

San Luis Sourdough
San Luis Obispo, CA

For great results, try serving this on thin slices of toasted San Luis Sourdough bread.

1 tablespoon butter

1 tablespoon olive oil

1/2 pound porcini mushrooms

1 cup beef stock

1/2 teaspoon Spice Hunter Italian seasoning

toast

salt and fresh ground pepper to taste

goat cheese at room temperature

COFFEE BRAISED BEEF

3 tablespoons oil
2 pounds braising beef, cubed
2 large onions, peeled and sliced
2 cloves garlic, crushed
2 green peppers, seeded, sliced
1 ounce flour
$^{1}/_{4}$ pint dry white wine
$^{1}/_{2}$ pint black coffee
1 teaspoon dried oregano
salt and fresh-milled black pepper

Brown beef in heated oil. Remove meat, leaving oil in pan. Sauté onions, garlic, and peppers in remaining oil. Sprinkle flour over vegetables and cook for 2 or 3 minutes. Gradually stir in wine and coffee and bring to boil, stirring constantly. Add oregano, salt, pepper, and cooked beef. Cover and simmer gently for $1^{1}/_{2}$ to 2 hours, or until beef is very tender. Add seasoning to taste.

Central Coast Coffee Roasting Company
Los Osos, CA

This casserole is best when kept overnight and reheated.

CALIFORNIA MID-STATE BEERFEST

ATASCADERO

9

Annual. September date varies.

It's time to break the standard six-pack habit.

When you get to town, ask anyone to point you in the direction of the impressive Atascadero War Memorial Building. It's in the Sunken Gardens of this building that the California Mid-State Beerfest is held. The building was constructed, in 1918, by Atascadero founder, Edward G. Lewis. It was Lewis's intent to develop a colony that would be totally self-sufficient.

According to festival organizers, this one-day event is the only beer festival ever organized by type of beer rather than by brewery. With more than seventy participating breweries, the beer tasting allows the consumer to compare beers of the same style. From pale ales to stout, from browns to wheat beer, you'll have the opportunity to taste your varietal preferences side by side.

Patrons are given a program describing each of the beers. Then, with a little tasting, you can judge what your individual taste buds prefer.

This annual event features the Atascadero Elks Club tri-tip barbecue and various concessionaires displaying and selling everything from glass etchings to cigars. During the feasting and sampling, attendees are entertained by a variety of musical performers.

(Continued)

It's a sight to behold, as you stroll among the beer booths. You'll no doubt be impressed by the warm hospitality, community gardens, and the varied and impressive selection of beers. Advance tickets include admission, souvenir beer glass, program, and taste tickets.

This unique event is sponsored by the chamber of commerce, Atascadero Business Improvement Association, and the local Elks Club. You'll find the city of Atascadero located on U.S. Highway 101 midway between San Luis Obispo and Paso Robles.

BUBBLY BEER BREAD

3 cups sifted self-rising flour

2 tablespoons sugar

1/2 teaspoon salt

1/2 teaspoon white pepper

12 ounces beer

Mix all dry ingredients in a medium bowl. Mix well. Add beer and stir until well combined; pour into a greased bread pan. Bake at 350° for 40 to 45 minutes until bread is lightly browned on top and sounds hollow when tapped. Butter top after removing from oven. Cool.

For variety add one or more of the following: 1/4 cup sun dried tomatoes; 2 tablespoons diced onion; 1 tablespoon minced garlic; 1/4 teaspoon Herbs de Provençe. I found this handwritten recipe tucked inside a thrift shop vintage cookbook.

BRADY'S BEAUTIFUL BEER BASTING SAUCE

1/2 cup flat pale ale

2 tablespoons vinegar

1 1/2 tablespoons Worcestershire sauce

1/3 cup firmly packed brown sugar

2/3 cup chili sauce

2 tablespoons honey

2 tablespoons sesame seeds

pinch cayenne pepper

Combine all ingredients in sauce pan, heat, and stir until sugar dissolves. Makes about 2 cups of sauce.

Brady Cherry
Atascadero, CA

Attend the California Mid-State Beerfest and try out several of the ales before selecting a favorite to use in this recipe.

DIPPING SHRIMP

Add beer to a large pot of water and bring to a rolling boil. While waiting for the water to boil, mix catsup, horseradish, and lemon juice together for the cocktail sauce. Plunge shrimp, all at once, into the boiling water and leave in for exactly 3 minutes. Drain shrimp and immediately cover with ice to stop the cooking process. When shrimp are cooled, peel and devein, leaving tail on. Arrange on a serving platter with the dish of cocktail sauce in the center. Refrigerate until serving time.

Gail Hobbs, recipe consultant
Ventura, CA

1/2 can beer

1/2 cup catsup

1 tablespoon horseradish

squeeze fresh lemon

1/2 pound large raw shrimp (16/21-count), if frozen, thaw

ice

GERMAN POTATO SALAD

8 large potatoes

3/4 pound bacon

3/4 cup Shields' Channel Islands Wheat Beer

3/4 cup finely chopped green onion

1/3 cup finely chopped celery

1 teaspoon salt

2 tablespoons brown sugar

2 teaspoons black pepper

1/4 cup parsley, chopped

Wash and scrub potatoes. Do not peel. Slice very thin. Fry bacon crisp. Remove to paper towel and drain. Crumble bacon and set aside. Remove most of the bacon drippings from the pan, add potatoes, beer, and rest of ingredients except parsley and bacon. Bring to a boil, cover, and simmer until potatoes are tender, about 20 minutes. Add bacon, stir gently, and put into serving dish. Garnish with parsley.

Shields Brewing Company
Ventura, CA

Cooking the potatoes in beer and seasonings allows them to absorb most of the moisture and retain nutrients better.

CELEBRATION OF HARVEST

SANTA BARBARA COUNTY

10

Annual. Mid-October Saturday.

There's no doubt about it. Santa Barbara is one of California's most popular destinations. In no small part, it's due to the area's delicious culinary offerings and fine wine pairings. To enjoy it all, you may want to plan your visit to coincide with the annual Celebration of Harvest.

Here's your chance to enjoy a celebration that features the county's thirty-four wineries as well as the foods prepared by outstanding area chefs.

In addition to wine and food tasting, you'll gain insightful information about local wine and wine making at interactive exhibits and displays detailing the many features of the industry. In addition, there are vineyard tours, musical entertainment, and the procession of scarecrows.

What's the scarecrow procession all about, you ask?

Many of the wineries and vineyards make scarecrows to decorate their booths at the event. Near the end, the scarecrows are paraded around the festival site to the sounds of musical entertainment. You'll have a great time (and a glass of wine or two) as you watch the fascinating march of the scarecrow sculptures compete for the perpetual trophy award.

(Continued)

In conjunction with the Celebration of Harvest, most wineries hold open houses and special activities. Winemaker dinners, tastings, and vineyard picnics are among the events scheduled. A few special events have included five-course meals matched with award-winning wines, wild game dinners, winemaker seminars and lectures, and barrel tastings of selected wines.

Worthy of note: The Santa Barbara County Vintner's Association, sponsor of the event, includes a designated driver program as part of the celebration.

Since this event sells out quickly, it's recommended you contact the association well in advance for details and reservations. When you do, you'll receive a free, full-color wine touring map, festival schedule, and reservation information.

No matter when you visit Santa Barbara County, you'll discover it to be a culinary mecca containing award-winning restaurants and the fastest-growing wine region in the world.

CRAB AND CHEDDAR FONDUE

Drain crabmeat well and flake. Toss together cheese and flour. In double boiler, heat wine until bubbles rise. Over low heat, add crab and cheese, $^1/_2$ cup at a time, stirring until cheese is melted after each addition. Transfer to fondue pot.

Gainey Vineyard
Santa Ynez, CA

Serve with toasted French bread cubes or vegetable dippers.

6 ounces fresh or frozen crabmeat (if frozen, thaw)

20 ounces cheddar cheese, shredded

2 tablespoons all-purpose flour

$1^1/_2$ cups Gainey Vineyard Johannisberg Riesling

CABERNET SAUVIGNON SAUCE

1 bottle Gainey Vineyard Cabernet Sauvignon

3 cups beef stock

1/2 cup chopped carrots

1/2 cup chopped celery

1 small onion, minced

2 shallots, minced

1/2 teaspoon parsley

1/2 teaspoon thyme

1 bay leaf

8 tablespoons butter

Combine all ingredients except butter in large saucepan. Simmer until liquid is reduced to 2 cups. This will take about 20 minutes. When reduced, purée in food processor or blender until smooth. Add butter in 8 equal pieces, whisking until blended. Heat thoroughly and serve over your favorite meat.

Gainey Vineyard
Santa Ynez, CA

This sauce is especially good poured over lamb or filet mignon.

ARUGULA SHRIMP FETTUCINE

6 to 8 ounces very fresh large raw shrimp

salt and freshly ground black pepper to taste

about 3 tablespoons extra virgin olive oil

3 ounces dry egg fettucine, cooked al dente in boiling salted water, drained

$^{1}/_{4}$ cup ripe tomatoes, peeled, seeded, drained, diced small

generous 2 cups arugula leaves (loosely pack to measure), bundled together and sliced $^{1}/_{4}$ inch thick

Peel, devein, rinse, and dry shrimp. Season with salt and pepper. Heat about 1 tablespoon oil in a medium-large or large heavy frying pan over medium heat. Add shrimp and cook, turning occasionally, until pink and firm and barely opaque throughout; remove from heat. Mix hot pasta with salt and pepper to season and enough oil to cloak very well, about 2 tablespoons. Add shrimp and tomatoes with all juices and arugula. Gently toss to mingle. Serve immediately.

Shirley Sarvis
Sanford Winery
Buellton, CA

This recipe was created especially to serve with Sanford Winery 1992 Sauvignon Blanc.

MEDITERRANEAN PASTA WITH CALIFORNIA PISTACHIOS

2 cups onion cut into narrow wedges

2 tablespoons olive oil (can use oil drained from tomatoes)

2 tablespoons minced garlic

1 tablespoon flour

1½ cups dry white wine

1 cup California pistachios

1 cup sun-dried tomatoes packed in olive oil

1 tablespoon dry basil

1 tablespoon dry oregano

½ cup minced fresh parsley (optional)

1 cup grated Parmesan cheese

8 ounces angel hair pasta (capellini), broken up

In a 12-inch skillet, sauté onions in oil for 5 to 10 minutes, or until cooked through. Add garlic and sauté 1 minute more. Stir flour into onions and garlic, add wine and cook. Stir until mixture comes to a boil and thickens slightly. Add pistachios, tomatoes, basil, oregano, and parsley to pan and heat through. Keep warm.

Cook pasta in boiling water 3 to 5 minutes or just until tender (note package directions); drain.

Combine pasta and sauce, sprinkle with cheese, and toss lightly. Offer additional cheese as garnish, if desired.

California Pistachio Commission
Fresno, CA

CELEBRATION OF HERBS

SQUAW VALLEY

Annual. Last weekend in April.

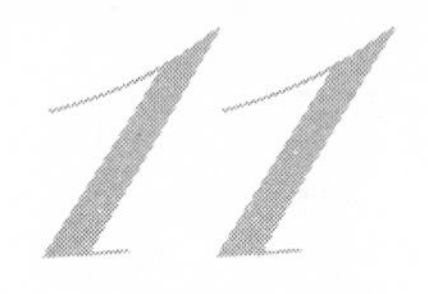

Here's your chance to celebrate both the rhythm of the earth's changing seasons and garden-fresh herbs to perk up your meals. The Celebration of Herbs is held in a peaceful landscape, surrounded by fragrant herbs and flowers. In a garden-lover's paradise, you'll discover food, verse, and song. You'll get a chance to smell and taste the splendors of lavender, sage, rosemary, and thyme.

This festival is like no other. It's small, casual, and rewarding. You won't find a carnival, a parade, or trumpets blaring. Instead, you'll be surrounded by beauty in a small, private garden atmosphere. The celebration is guaranteed to bring peace to your soul and joy to your heart. If you're lucky, you'll leave with a little thyme on your hands.

The Squaw Valley Herb Garden is owned by Rosemary Nachtigall and T.D. Friesen, two California artists in love with the land. They design, cook, and create among hundreds of herbs and old-fashioned flowers.

(Continued)

Several special weekend celebrations are held throughout the year at the gardens. The Celebration of Wildflowers takes place the last weekend in March, the Lavender Harvest is the second weekend in June, the Celebration of Spice occurs the last weekend in June, and the Earthdance Celebration is held in October. Don't be surprised if you find yourself wanting to attend each of these unique and special feastings.

If you prefer small to large, peaceful to raucous, and simple to tumultuous, these celebrations may be exactly the kind of observances you want to share and experience. The community and the gardens are small. The celebrations are personal and relaxed. Reservations are highly recommended for all celebrations.

You don't want to mistake the small hamlet of Squaw Valley for its larger namesake near Lake Tahoe. This Squaw Valley is situated about 30 miles east of Fresno, and 20 miles west of Sequoia and Kings Canyon national parks.

POTATOES TARRAGON

Layer potatoes in a large buttered baking dish. In a saucepan add evaporated milk to butter, salt and pepper, and thin with a small amount of milk or water. When butter is melted, remove from heat. Sprinkle grated cheese over potatoes and add sauce. Sprinkle tarragon over casserole and cover with extra cheese. Cover casserole with foil, poke a few fork holes to release moisture, and bake at 350° for 30 minutes. Uncover and brown at 400° for several minutes, if desired. Garnish with a touch of fresh tarragon and serve.

Squaw Valley Herb Gardens
Squaw Valley, CA

6 to 8 medium potatoes, peeled, cut in thin slices

1/2 can evaporated milk

1/2 stick butter

salt and pepper to taste

milk or water (for thinning)

1 to 2 cups grated mozzarella cheese

1/4 cup chopped fresh tarragon medium-fine

ROSEMARY'S SAGED FRYBREAD

3 cups self-rising flour, plus 1 cup for shaping tortillas

$2^1/_2$ cups milk

8 large sage leaves, snipped into small strips

canola oil

Place 3 cups of flour into a bowl. Warm milk on low heat and stir in sage. Add milk to flour and stir into a soft, smooth batter. Keep dough on the soft side. (You can always add more flour to the batter, but once the batter becomes too stiff you will have rock-like frybread.) Shape into small hand-size balls and let rise. Keep 1 or more cups of flour handy to flour the board and use in patting out the tortillas. Pat out excess flour while shaping tortilla and gently put into hot oil in frying pan. Fry each side until golden brown. Lay on paper towels to remove excess oil.

Variations: Rosemary leaves may be substituted for sage, providing a flavorful taste. A teaspoon or more of your favorite red chilies or chopped garlic adds spice too.

Squaw Valley Herb Gardens
Squaw Valley, CA

Try with cinnamon-sugar, or with grated cheese, refried beans, Spanish rice, fresh tomato salsa, and sour cream.

SAGE PASTA

Melt in a saucepan, 1 pint heavy cream and 1 cube of butter. Bring to a very slight boil, where tiny bubbles form around the edge of the pan. Add 1/2 cup fresh grated Parmesan cheese, 1/4 teaspoon (or more) fresh grated nutmeg, and 1 cup fresh, not too finely chopped sage leaves. Cook until tiny bubbles form around the pan again. Stir often throughout the preparation. Toss over cooked fettucini and serve at once.

Sycamore Gazette
Sycamore Farms
Paso Robles, CA

The Sycamore Farms newsletter editor recalls, "A customer last Fall bought a gallon of sage, so I asked her what in the world was she going to do with all the sage. This is the recipe she gave me, which was an old Italian family recipe from her aunt."

1 pint heavy cream
1 cube or 1/2 cup butter
1/2 cup grated Parmesan cheese
1/4 teaspoon grated nutmeg
1 cup chopped sage leaves
fettucini

A DIFFERENT PESTO SAUCE

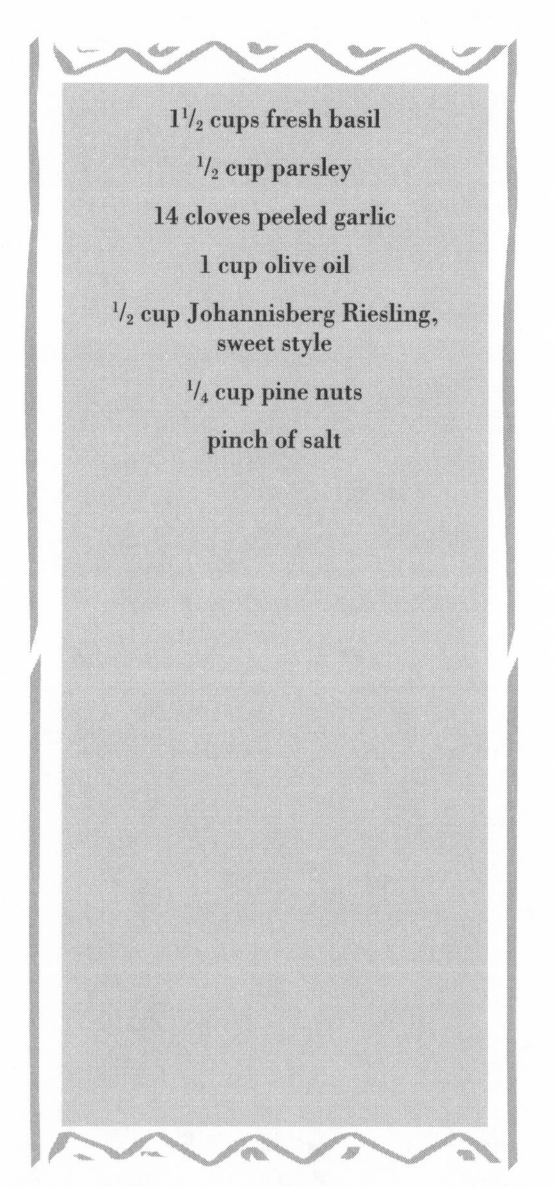

Place basil, parsley, and garlic (all 14 cloves) in a food processor fitted with a steel blade. Turn on processor and add olive oil in a steady stream through feed tube. Add wine, pine nuts, and salt. Process until smooth.

Patricia Ballard, author
Fine Wine in Food and Wine in Everyday Cooking
Paso Robles

CELEBRATION OF WESTERN CULTURE

KERN COUNTY

Annual. September date varies.

In California, it seems everyone loves to munch and sun simultaneously. This is your chance to take a break from the heat and satisfy your need for fabulous flavors.

The Kern County CattleWomen organize and host this annual celebration of good taste. The event is held on the Tracy Ranch, one of Kern County's few remaining pioneer ranches. For directions, please contact the CattleWomen in advance.

Friendly company and a social atmosphere will remind you of an old-time ranch party. Specialties of this one-day event include a silent auction, horse racing, roping, branding demonstrations, backcountry horse demonstrations, and the infamous cow plop. In the evening, the full, finger-licking, and rich flavors of a sizzling western barbecue and phenomenal libations fill the air and the stomach. After the meal, you may want to work off a few calories by dancing the night away to the sounds of lively music and good, heartland entertainment.

When it's all over, you'll have been a part of a truly western-style party. In addition, you'll have experienced a variety of traditional victuals and some of the rich heritage of the West, as well as gained plenty of wisdom about Kern County's formidable cattle industry.

ORANGE SALSA BEEF

Marinade

$^2/_3$ cup frozen orange juice concentrate, thawed

$^1/_2$ cup tequila

$^1/_3$ cup fresh lime juice

1 tablespoon olive oil

2 tablespoons chopped fresh ginger

2 medium cloves garlic, crushed

1 teaspoon salt

1 teaspoon dried oregano leaves, crushed

$^1/_4$ teaspoon ground red pepper

$1^1/_2$ pounds well-trimmed boneless beef top round steak or other lean beef such as sirloin, cut 1-inch thick

Orange Salsa

2 oranges, peeled and cut into $^1/_2$-inch pieces

1 small red or white onion, chopped

1 jalapeño pepper, seeded and finely chopped

$^1/_3$ cup chopped fresh cilantro

2 to 3 tablespoons fresh lime juice

2 tablespoons olive oil

$^1/_2$ teaspoon salt

$^1/_2$ teaspoon dried oregano leaves, crushed

cilantro sprigs and lime wedges for garnish

Combine orange juice, tequila, lime juice, oil, ginger, garlic, salt, oregano, and pepper. Place marinade and steak in plastic bag or marinating container. Securely close and turn to coat meat. Place in refrigerator for 4 to 24 hours.

Prepare orange salsa by combining and mixing all ingredients. Set aside to flavor.

Place steak on grill over medium coals. Grill 22 to 26 minutes for medium-rare to medium, turning once. Remove steak to carving board. Let stand 10 minutes. Carve steak crosswise into thin slices; arrange on serving platter. Garnish with cilantro sprigs and lime wedges. Serve with Orange Salsa.

Lynelle Echeverria, president
Kern County CattleWomen
Kern County, CA

FAJITA SANDWICH

Marinate beef in picante sauce for at least 1 hour. Drain and cook in frying pan until done. Sauté peppers and onion together. Assemble as follows on foil large enough to wrap a loaf of bread. Slice bread lengthwise and scoop out some bread from each side. Layer beef and all other ingredients in order except melted butter on bottom half of loaf. Replace top half and drizzle with melted butter or margarine. Wrap and seal in foil. Bake at 350° for 20 minutes. Cut in slices and serve with guacamole, salsa, and sour cream.

Alice Bowen
CattleWoman
Kern County, CA

1½ to 2 pounds beef, such as tri-tip or round steak strips, cut into bite-size pieces

1 cup picante sauce

⅓ cup diced bell pepper

⅓ cup diced onion

1 long loaf French or sour dough bread, sliced length-wise

⅔ cup grated mozzarella cheese

⅓ cup grated cheddar cheese

1 small can sliced olives

¼ cup melted butter or margarine

guacamole, salsa, and sour cream for garnish

ITALIAN BEEF STIR-FRY

1 pound beef round tip steaks

2 or 3 cloves garlic, crushed

1 tablespoon olive oil

salt and pepper

1 small zucchini, thinly sliced

1 yellow crookneck squash, thinly sliced

1 cup cherry tomato halves

1/4 cup reduced-calorie bottled Italian salad dressing

2 cups hot cooked spaghetti

1 tablespoon grated Parmesan cheese

Cut beef crosswise into 1-inch strips, cut each strip crosswise in half. Cook and stir garlic in oil in large non-stick skillet over medium-high heat 1 minute. Add beef strips (1/2 at a time), stir-fry 1 to 2 minutes. Season with salt and pepper. Remove with slotted spoon, keep warm. Add zucchini and crookneck squash to same skillet, stir-fry 2 or 3 minutes or until crisp-tender. Return beef to skillet, add tomato halves and dressing, and heat through. Serve beef mixture over hot spaghetti, sprinkle with Parmesan cheese, and serve with toasted sourdough garlic bread.

Kate Hunter
CattleWoman
from *30 Meals in 30 Minutes. Beef. It's What's For Dinner.*
Kern County, CA

SALSA BEEF

To prepare salsa, combine tomatoes, olives, onion, lime juice, jalapeño chili, cilantro, and garlic. Mix well. Coarsely crush 1/2 cup tortilla chips and set aside.

In a large bowl, mix steak with salt and pepper. Heat oil in a non-stick frying pan over medium-high heat. Add meat and cook, stirring, until done to your liking. Remove pan from heat, transfer meat to a bowl, keep warm. Add salsa to drippings in pan, cook over medium heat until slightly thickened and hot, 1 to 2 minutes. Stir meat into salsa. Spoon meat mixture over lettuce to serve. Top with sour cream and sprinkle with crushed tortilla chips. Garnish with cilantro sprigs and offer remaining chips.

California Olive Industry
Fresno, CA

Salsa

2 medium tomatoes, chopped, well drained

1/2 cup coarsely chopped California ripe olives

1/4 cup thinly sliced green onions

squeeze of lime juice

1 small fresh jalapeño chili, seeded, finely chopped

1 tablespoon finely chopped cilantro

1 clove garlic, minced

about 4 cups tortilla chips

1 pound lean boneless top sirloin steak, fat trimmed, cut into 1/2-inch pieces

1/4 teaspoon salt

1/8 teaspoon pepper

2 teaspoons salad oil

about 8 cups finely shredded lettuce

1/2 cup sour cream

cilantro sprigs (optional)

CLAM FESTIVAL

PISMO BEACH

Annual. Third weekend in October.

What's a beach without clams? For more than fifty years, the annual Clam Festival has celebrated Pismo Beach's reputation as the clam capital of the world. The famed mollusk is celebrated with a parade, plenty of food, craft booths, a chowder competition, a carnival, clam digging, and live entertainment.

If you're expecting plenty of clam dishes, you won't be disappointed. Chowder chefs face off during the annual battle for the title of best clam chowder in Pismo Beach. It's great fun to join in the rousing competition as a variety of local restaurants prepare their perennial favorites featuring special blends of ingredients. You'll be amazed at what goes on as the chowder heats up.

The entertaining, hometown festival parade along Dolliver Street features all kinds of clam-related entries. You'll feast your eyes upon clam-decorated floats, clam-dressed kids, clam-bands, and enough clam shells to satisfy the needs of any clammer.

Several years ago the festival's mascots, Sam and Pam Clam, finally tied the knot at a wedding befitting the festival. Accompanied by reveling festival-goers, their escorts, and minister, the two joined their clammy hands together, spoke their vows, and committed to live in marital bliss until the end of time. Now, with their kids in tow, the family continues to entertain throughout the event. Bring your camera.

The Clam family loves having their picture taken and welcomes you to join them for a family portrait.

In keeping with the family theme, a carnival delights everyone of all ages with ongoing rides, sideshows, and competitive games. From the carnival site, it's a short walk out to the pier where celebrants watch the beach volleyball tournament, sand sculpture competition, waiter/waitress contest, and the famous clam dig. If you're lucky, you may walk off with one of the prizes.

In addition to a wide array of events and tantalizing aromas, the Pismo Clam Festival produces a festival cookbook filled with tasty treats. You can purchase a copy at the festival information booth.

Pismo Beach is located on California's central coast at the junction of California Highways 1 and 101.

RED CLAM SAUCE

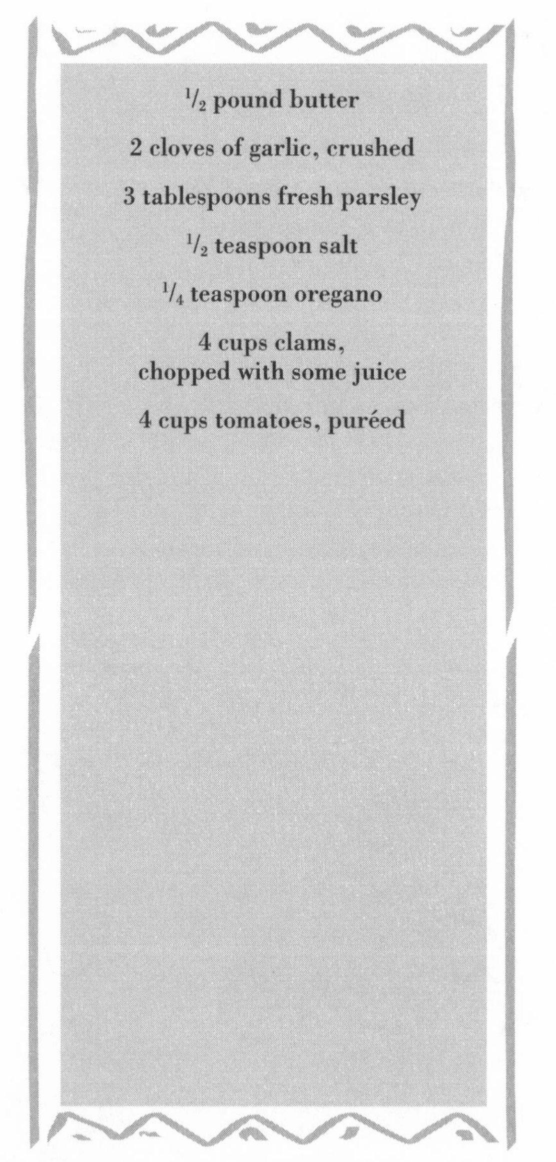

$^{1}/_{2}$ pound butter

2 cloves of garlic, crushed

3 tablespoons fresh parsley

$^{1}/_{2}$ teaspoon salt

$^{1}/_{4}$ teaspoon oregano

4 cups clams,
chopped with some juice

4 cups tomatoes, puréed

Melt butter, sauté garlic and parsley. Add remaining ingredients and simmer for 15 minutes. Serve with linguine or fettucini.

Diane Carpenter
Clemenza's Pizza and Torpedo Factory
Pismo Beach, CA

SEA CAPTAIN'S CLAM CHOWDER

In a large saucepan, fry bacon or salt pork until crisp. Pour off fat, add onion, potatoes, clam juice, and 1 cup water. Use water in which clams were steamed, if possible. Cook on medium heat until potatoes are tender, about 10 minutes. Add clams, half-and-half, and heat but do not boil. Add salt and pepper to taste. Thicken if desired.

Niki Hardt, festival volunteer
Oxnard, CA

Niki has long dug clams at Pismo Beach. She's prepared her clam chowder for me, and I loved it!

3 slices of bacon or salt pork

1/2 cup chopped onion

2 cups peeled, diced potatoes

8 ounce bottled clam juice

1 cup water

12 steamed Pismo clams or 2 6 1/2-ounce cans of chopped clams

1 1/2 cups half-and-half

salt and pepper to taste

PISMO CLAM TACOS

raw clam strips
(1/2 ounce per taco)

fish batter

vegetable oil

corn tortillas

crushed ripe avocado

salt

pepper

powered garlic

cumin

chopped red or green cabbage

salsa

Garnishes

chopped tomatoes

chopped onion

cilantro

diced radish

lime

Dip raw clams in fish batter and deep fry in vegetable oil at 365° for 1 minute or until clam strips are golden brown. Warm 2 corn tortillas on griddle until soft and lay one on top of the other. Butter the warm tortilla with guacamole (crushed avocado, seasoned with teaspoon of salt, pepper, garlic, and cumin). Place the fried clam strips across the middle of the tortillas. Top the clams with shredded green or red cabbage. Top cabbage with salsa and garnishes. Serve with a squeeze of lime.

Jalapeños Taco Hut
Pismo Beach, CA

CLAMS OR OYSTERS ON THE HALF SHELL

Open the clams or oysters, leaving them in the deep half of the shell. Place 4 to 6 on each serving plate. To keep them appetizingly cold, set them on crushed ice. Serve with your favorite cocktail sauce.

Bob Carter
Oxnard, CA

This is my favorite way to prepare and serve a tempting appetizer.

clams or oysters
cocktail sauce
crushed ice

FRENCH FESTIVAL

SANTA BARBARA

Annual. July Bastille Day weekend.

Ooh la la! It's a sunny Bastille Day, and everyone has the urge to be French for the weekend. Smiling families dine at sidewalk cafes and tables with checkered tablecloths and umbrellas. Starry-eyed couples toast each other with wine. Artists wearing berets paint at their easels. The air is filled with music, laughter, and the tempting aromas of French cuisine.

Think you've suddenly been whisked off to France? Actually, it's Santa Barbara, and you're enjoying the sights, sounds, food, and *joie de vivre* at the largest French celebration in the western United States. You'll be tempted by dozens of chefs preparing fine French food—everything from crepes to Cajun, from café au lait to decadent desserts and pastries.

Music fills the air, and dazzling entertainment includes can can dancers, Moroccan belly dancers, grand opera, Cajun and classical groups, and cabaret music in the tradition of Edith Piaf and Maurice Chevalier. Wandering mimes, jugglers, and accordion players perform throughout the crowd. Kids are held spellbound by puppets, storytellers, and a wading pool.

Under a huge Eiffel Tower replica, you'll discover a continent of displays that include classic French automobiles, flower markets, and a Montmartre artists' colony. Who knows, you may win in the Napoleon Look-Alike Contest. Prizes are awarded for Best All-Around Napoleon, Best Josephine, Best Little Kid Napoleon, and Best Reason for Hand-in-Shirt.

To reach the free Santa Barbara French Festival, take the Pueblo or Mission exit from U.S. Highway 101 and follow the signs to beautiful Oak Park.

RATATOUILLE

Chop vegetables into bite-size chunks. Sauté onion and garlic until softened, a minute or two, in half of the olive oil. Add everything else, simmer 25 to 30 minutes, until all the vegetables have softened. Serve warm or at room temperature with crusty French bread as an hors d'oeuvre, main, or side dish.

French Festival Committee
Santa Barbara, CA

The vegetables for this Provençal stew are best when picked fresh and ripe from your own garden, or selected at your farmers' market. Exact proportions are not critical. Provençal purists would demand that each veggie be cooked separately, then combined, but this version is easy and delicious.

3 large vine-ripened tomatoes, regular or Roma, (approximately 1½ pounds)

2 medium bell peppers, green, red, yellow, or combination (approximately 1 pound)

1 zucchini, green, yellow, or combination (approximately 1 pound)

1 medium eggplant (approximately 1 pound)

1 yellow onion (approximately 1 pound)

2 to 5 cloves garlic, crushed or chopped

2 to 3 tablespoons virgin olive oil

chopped fresh basil

salt and pepper to taste

Optional, but not traditional: rosemary, parsley, marjoram, thyme, and a glug of red wine

FRENCH ONION SOUP

3 to 4 tablespoons butter

1 to 2 tablespoons oil

6 to 7 cups thinly sliced onions

1 teaspoon salt

1/2 teaspoon sugar

3 tablespoons flour

2 quarts chicken stock

bay leaf

sage

1/2 cup wine, optional

salt and pepper, optional

croutons

grated Swiss or Swiss/ Parmesan mixture

Melt butter with oil in a large kettle. Add onions, cook uncovered over low heat for 15 to 20 minutes, stirring occasionally. Add salt and sugar and cook 15 to 20 minutes more, stirring occasionally. Sprinkle on flour and cook 2 to 3 minutes, stirring, to brown. In another pan, bring stock to a simmer, then pour it over the onions. Add herbs to taste. Add wine if desired. Simmer on low heat, partially covered, another 20 to 30 minutes. Add salt and pepper if needed.

To serve: place croutons in bowl, ladle on soup, sprinkle on cheese. Or, ladle soup into ovenproof bowls, top with croutons, sprinkle on cheese, and place under broiler until cheese melts and bubbles. Serve with French bread.

French Festival Committee
Santa Barbara, CA

FRUIT FRAPPÉ

peeled bananas, melon chunks, and whole berries, rinsed and patted dry

milk and/or orange juice

crushed ice (optional)

Place fruit on cookie tray and freeze until solid. Store in freezer in plastic bag. Put frozen fruit in blender. Frozen bananas will make the drink creamy like a milk shake. Add milk and/or juice and add crushed ice if desired. Blend. Serve in a tall glass or wine glass . . . with a spoon if it's really thick.

Guy deMangeion
"The Berry Man"
Santa Barbara, CA

If you make this recipe extra thick, it can be served as a dessert.

PISSALADIÈRE

Onion Pizza

1 envelope yeast

1 cup warm water

1 teaspoon sugar

3 cups unbleached flour

1 teaspoon salt

4 tablespoons olive oil

3 large onions, sliced thin

3 to 5 cloves of garlic, crushed or chopped

salt and pepper to taste

cornmeal

anchovies or anchovy paste (optional)

Herbes de Provençe (or use any combination of basil, oregano, marjoram, thyme, or rosemary)

black olives

Activate yeast in 1/4 cup warm water and 1 teaspoon sugar. Blend into rest of water and add flour, 1 teaspoon salt, and 1 tablespoon oil. Knead until resilient, cover, and set aside in warm spot to rise until doubled, about an hour, but longer is better.

Sauté onions and garlic in 2 tablespoons oil until softened and colored, but don't overcook. Salt and pepper to taste. Punch down dough, stretch and roll from 1/8 to 1/4 inch thick, transfer to baking pan sprinkled with cornmeal, rub 1 tablespoon olive oil on top, and let rest 15 to 20 minutes.

Preheat oven to very hot, 400° to 500°. Roll out dough to fit your pizza pan. Distribute onion and garlic mixture and anchovies in an interesting checkerboard pattern over top of dough. If using anchovy paste, rub it over top of dough before adding onion mixture. Sprinkle on Herbes de Provençe, add olives to your taste. Put in middle rack of oven until crust is raised and crisp on bottom. Serve hot or at room temperature.

Steve Hoegerman
Santa Barbara French Festival
Santa Barbara, CA

FRESH FRUIT FESTIVAL

Reedley

Annual. Fourth weekend in June.

Plums. Strawberries. Peaches. Pears. Nectarines. Apples. Melons. Apricots. Kiwis. Figs. These and other fresh fruits take center stage at Reedley's annual extravaganza celebrating the area's rich fruit harvest. The event is colorful, fun, and festive, and you'll be dazzled by the choice of foods, entertainment, and exhibits. A variety of interesting displays are provided by many of the major fruit-marketing organizations. Of course, you'll want to take advantage of the ample chance to taste the tempting morsels offered by local growers.

Held on the campus of Kings River Community College, a motorized trolley takes you back and forth from the festival to Reedley's turn-of-the-century downtown. In town, several of the restaurants feature special fresh fruit dishes. Kings River Community College address: 995 North Reed Avenue, Reedley.

Back at the festival site, you won't want to miss out on two special contests: pie baking and watermelon eating. They're fun for the entire family. Then, take a walk through the art and craft area, exhibits, displays, demonstrations, and workshops. Just in case you haven't had your fill of fresh fruit, you'll have a chance to pick up plenty of brochures and recipes to take home with you.

Plan your trip so you'll have plenty of time to sample the foods, ride the trolley, and enjoy the sounds of some mighty fine live entertainment.

PEAR-PEPPER SALSA

2 fresh Bartlett pears, pared, cored, diced

1/3 cup diced red bell pepper

1/3 cup golden raisins

2 green onions, thinly sliced

1 fresh jalapeño pepper, minced or 1 tablespoon canned diced jalapeño

1 tablespoon white wine vinegar

2 teaspoons minced ginger root or 1/2 teaspoon ground ginger

8 flour tortillas, quarters or strips, warmed

In medium bowl, combine all ingredients except tortillas. Cover and refrigerate. Spoon onto tortilla quarters.

Reedley Fresh Fruit Festival
Reedley, CA

This salsa is a low-calorie topping great on grilled chicken, pork, fish, and quesadillas.

DESSERT FRUIT PIZZA

1 sheet (12-inch square) frozen puff pastry, thawed

1 ounce mozzarella cheese, shredded

1/2 cup ricotta cheese

1/4 cup golden raisins

2 tablespoons chopped walnuts

1/2 teaspoon ground cinnamon

1/2 teaspoon ground nutmeg

1 fresh nectarine, pitted, sliced

1 fresh Bartlett pear, cored, sliced

2 plums, pitted, sliced

3 tablespoons orange marmalade, warmed

Preheat oven to 400°. Place pastry on large baking pan; fold edges under to form ridge. Sprinkle with mozzarella. Top with small dollops of ricotta. Sprinkle with raisins, nuts, and spices. Arrange fruit on top. Drizzle with marmalade. Bake 20 to 25 minutes or until pastry is puffed and brown.

Reedley Fresh Fruit Festival
Reedley, CA

CALIFORNIA APPLE SNACKS

Apple Melt

California apples

English muffins

cheese

cherry tomatoes, parsley, sliced olives, pickle slices, or chopped onions

Apple Wedges

California apples

cinnamon and sugar

honey or peanut butter

coconut or cornflakes

cheese or ham slices

Apple Melt: Cut your favorite California apple crosswise to make rings with a star in the center. Use a small cookie cutter or melon baller to remove the star. Top English muffin halves with slices of cheese and microwave on high for a few seconds until the cheese is melted. Top with apple slices. Fill centers of apple slices with cherry tomatoes, parsley, sliced olives, pickle slices, or chopped onions.

Apple Wedges: Wedges of California apple are good plain, sprinkled with cinnamon and sugar, dipped in honey or peanut butter, rolled in coconut or cornflake crumbs, or wrapped in cheese or ham slices.

California Apple Commission
Fresno, CA

GRAPEFRUIT FESTIVAL

Borrego Springs

Annual. Third weekend in April.

16

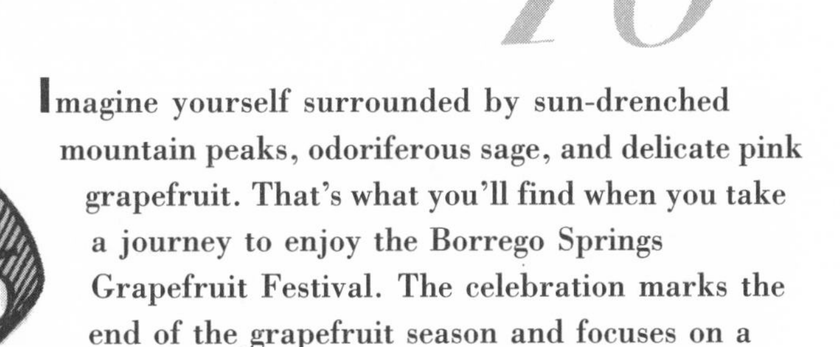

Imagine yourself surrounded by sun-drenched mountain peaks, odoriferous sage, and delicate pink grapefruit. That's what you'll find when you take a journey to enjoy the Borrego Springs Grapefruit Festival. The celebration marks the end of the grapefruit season and focuses on a banquet of foods, arts and crafts, entertainment, and events held at nearby restaurants and resorts.

The two-day festival is held in the city's Christmas Circle Park in the center of town. You'll get a kick out of tasting a variety of grapefruit-dominated foods. Be sure you pick up a sack or two of the local fruit and take it home with you.

Although many people consider the grapefruit a breakfast staple, when breakfast is over it's time to hit the road and enjoy the unexpected. You'll be amazed at the variety of tasty dishes that can be made using the nutritious citrus fruit. While you are at the festival, pick up a grapefruit cookbook. It features dozens of interesting and tempting recipes suitable for any meal of the day.

If you can, schedule a couple of days for enjoying the festival and the surrounding desert state park. If it's your nature, take along your bicycle, hiking boots, photographic equipment, and binoculars. You'll want to stay long enough to enjoy it all.

All recipes in this section were contributed by Borrego Springs Grapefruit Festival.

GRAPEFRUIT AND CRAB SALAD

<u>Sour Cream Mayonnaise Dressing</u>

2 egg yolks

1 teaspoon dry mustard

$^1/_2$ teaspoon salt

1 cup salad oil

2 tablespoons lemon juice

$^1/_2$ cup sour cream

butter lettuce leaves

2 cups crabmeat (about 1 pound)

2 pink grapefruit

1 avocado

lemon juice

$^1/_2$ cup pomegranate seeds (optional)

Prepare dressing first. Beat egg yolks with dry mustard and salt using a wire whip or an electric mixer, then gradually beat in salad oil, adding it drop by drop. When all the oil is incorporated, mix in lemon juice. Stir in sour cream. Makes about $1^1/_2$ cups.

Arrange a bed of lettuce leaves on four salad plates. Place a mound of crabmeat in center of each plate. Peel grapefruit and cut into sections, discarding white membrane. Peel and slice avocado, dip slices in lemon juice to prevent darkening. Arrange grapefruit and avocado in radiating spokes from the crab. If desired, sprinkle salads with pomegranate seeds. Top each salad with a spoonful of sour cream mayonnaise and pass additional dressing. Makes 4 servings.

GRAPEFRUIT CAESAR SALAD

In a food processor or blender, process all the ingredients for the dressing, except Parmesan cheese. Blend at high speed until well blended. Fold in cheese and chill. Makes $1^1/_2$ cups dressing.

Divide all ingredients attractively among 6 plates. Drizzle each with 1 tablespoon dressing.

Dressing

1 cup fat-free cottage cheese

$^1/_2$ teaspoon freshly ground pepper

$2^1/_2$ anchovies, rinsed well

$^1/_4$ cup water

$^1/_4$ cup skim milk

2 tablespoons fresh grapefruit juice

2 large cloves garlic, crushed

6 tablespoons light olive oil

$^1/_2$ cup freshly grated Parmesan cheese

Salad

1 head romaine lettuce, washed and trimmed

6 ounces shrimp, shelled and deveined

2 grapefruits, peeled and sectioned

GRAPEFRUIT-RAISIN COFFEE CAKE

1 grapefruit

2 cups biscuit mix

1/2 cup raisins

1/3 cup plus 2 tablespoons sugar

1/3 cup plus 1 tablespoon butter or margarine, melted

1/3 cup milk

1 egg, lightly beaten

1/2 teaspoon cinnamon

Peel and section grapefruit over bowl, reserving sections and 1/4 cup juice. Combine biscuit mix, raisins, and 1/3 cup sugar in large bowl. Add 1/3 cup melted butter, milk, egg, and reserved grapefruit juice. Mix just until blended. Spoon into lightly greased 8-inch square baking pan. Arrange grapefruit sections on top. Drizzle with remaining 1 tablespoon melted butter. Combine remaining 2 tablespoons sugar with cinnamon and sprinkle over cake. Bake at 400° for 30 minutes or until wooden toothpick inserted in center comes out clean. Serve warm.

GRECIAN FESTIVAL BY-THE-SEA

LONG BEACH

Annual. Labor Day weekend.

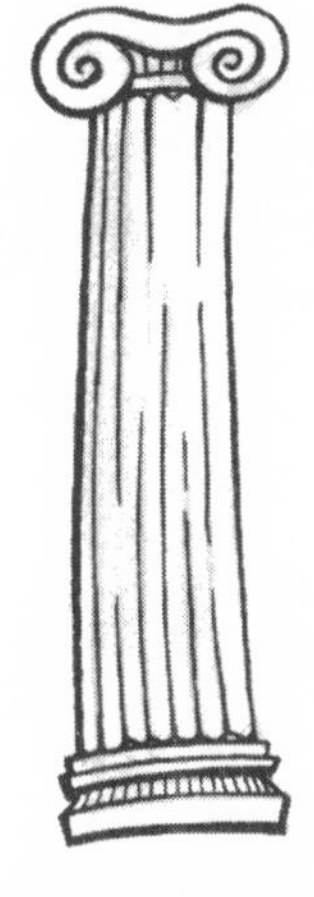

Gather up the kids, practice saying "Opa," and follow the Greek music to a three-day celebration at the Rainbow Lagoon in Long Beach. There's plenty of dancing, food, and entertainment during this annual Labor Day feast.

Your taste buds will savor the variety of Greek food and pastries available, including tiropetas, spanikopitas, Greek barbecued chicken, arni, loukomades, and baklava. You can buy individual food items or purchase an entire Greek dinner, depending on your personal food-tasting demands.

Greek cooking demonstrations are held at various times throughout the festival. Pay close attention and you'll likely learn why olive oil is used so heavily in much of Greek cooking. If you're lucky, you might even get a chance to taste some souvlaki, moussaka, or soupa avgolemono. No matter what the bill of fare, you'll go home happy, having enjoyed a day of ethnic diversity and cultural enrichment.

Some say that the Greeks invented entertainment. If this is so, this festival lives up to its roots. Continuous performances feature Greek dancers in traditional costumes. You may join in during Greek dancing lessons to the sounds of Greek music. Believe me, you'll have the time of your life.

A feature not found at most festivals is the showing of film and video programs. Provided by the Greek National Tourist Organization, the films allow the public to enjoy a vicarious visit to Greek temple ruins and other well-known landmarks and to learn more about the Greek people and their historic and contemporary lives and culture.

(Continued)

Greece is a seafaring nation, and the people are well known for their love of the sea, sailing, and fishing. It's not exactly like being there, but Rainbow Lagoon, located at Shoreline Drive and Linden Avenue, is as close to Greece as you can get without leaving California.

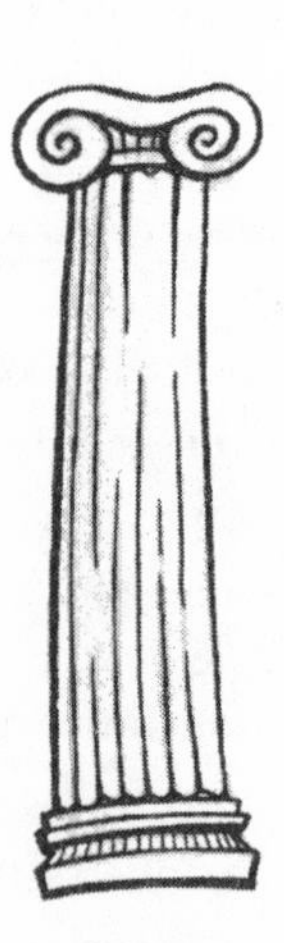

DOLMADAKIA

Stuffed Grape Leaves

Rinse grape leaves and remove stems. Separate and drain. Cook onions in olive oil until limp; add scallions, parsley, mint, dill, rice, lemon juice, salt, pepper, and 1 cup boiling water. Cover and simmer, stirring occasionally, until rice is tender. Do not overcook. Spread out grape leaves and place about 1 tablespoon rice filling in center of each leaf. Roll, starting from stem end, and fold in sides, ending with leaf point at top. Cut 4 lemons in round slices. Line saucepan with lemon slices, placing dolmades close together in layers. If any lemon slices remain, add to top of dolmades. Pour in 1 cup boiling water, place a heavy plate on top. Cover and cook over low heat for 30 minutes, cool. Arrange dolmades on platter. Cut 2 lemons in round slices and then cut slices in half. Decorate platter with the lemons. Serve hot or cold.

Grecian Festival by-the-Sea
Long Beach, CA

1 large jar grape leaves

3 pounds onions, chopped fine

1 pint olive oil

6 bunches scallions, finely chopped

1 cup finely chopped parsley

1 cup finely chopped mint

1 cup finely chopped dill weed

1 pound long grain rice

juice of 2 lemons

salt and pepper to taste

6 lemons

TIROPETA

Three-Cheese Crispy Appetizers

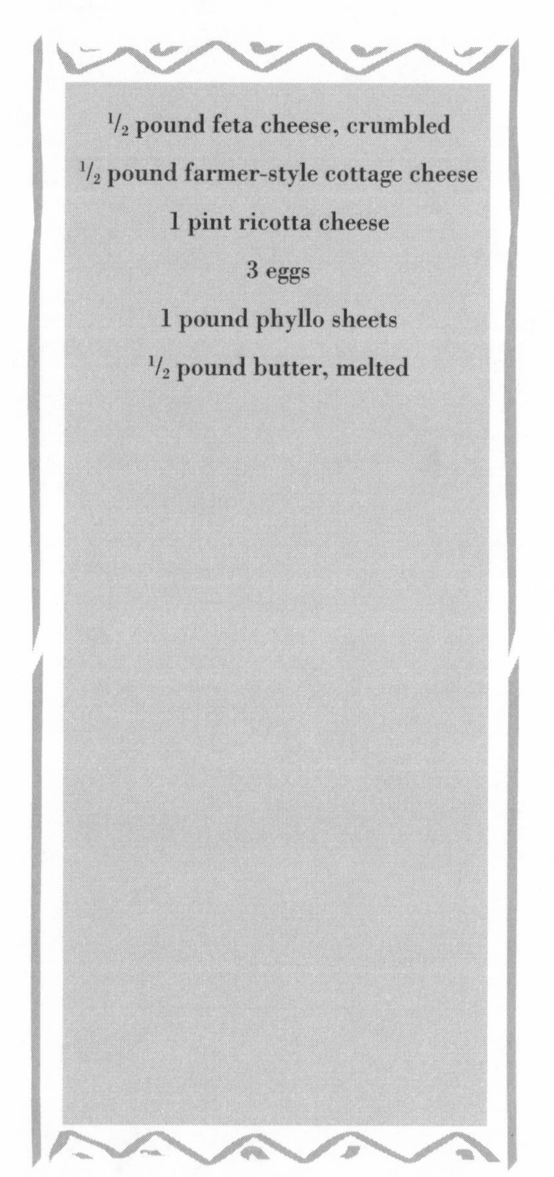

1/2 pound feta cheese, crumbled

1/2 pound farmer-style cottage cheese

1 pint ricotta cheese

3 eggs

1 pound phyllo sheets

1/2 pound butter, melted

Blend crumbled feta, cottage, and ricotta cheeses and mix thoroughly. Add eggs one at a time and mix well. Cut phyllo sheets into strips about 2 inches wide, and line them up on a board and brush with melted butter. Place 1 teaspoon of the filling on one end of pastry strip and fold corner over to make a triangle. Continue folding from side to side in the form of a triangle. Proceed until all filling and phyllo is used. Line the triangles in a buttered baking pan, brush generously with butter on top, and bake in moderate 350° oven, about 20 to 25 minutes or until golden brown.

Grecian Festival by-the-Sea
Long Beach, CA

Phyllo sheets may be found in your grocer's freezer.

SALATA HORIATIKE

Greek Country Salad

Cut romaine into small pieces and place in the bottom of a salad bowl. Top with the tomatoes, onion rings, sliced cucumber, feta cheese, anchovies, and olives. Combine the dressing ingredients in a shaker bottle and shake well. Pour the dressing over the salad and toss just before serving.

Grecian Festival by-the-Sea
Long Beach, CA

$^1/_2$ head romaine lettuce

2 tomatoes, cut into wedges

$^1/_2$ medium onion, sliced and separated into rings

$^1/_2$ cucumber, sliced

$^1/_4$ pound feta cheese, cut into $^3/_4$-inch chunks

3 anchovy fillets, if desired

8 calamata olives

Dressing

$^1/_3$ cup olive oil

$^1/_3$ cup wine vinegar

2 tablespoons water

$^1/_2$ teaspoon dried oregano

GREEK RICE TOSS

3 cups cooked rice

2 6-ounce jars marinated artichoke hearts, coarsely chopped, drained, liquid reserved

1 large tomato, seeded, chopped

1 medium cucumber, seeded, chopped

1 medium red onion, chopped

1 cup crumbled feta cheese

1 2¼-ounce can sliced black olives, drained

¼ cup fresh chopped parsley

1 tablespoon lemon juice

½ teaspoon oregano

½ teaspoon lemon pepper

lettuce leaves

Combine rice, artichoke hearts, tomato, cucumber, onion, cheese, olives, parsley, lemon juice, oregano, and lemon pepper. Chill 1 hour. Before serving, drizzle reserved artichoke liquid over salad. Spoon onto individual lettuce-lined plates. For a main dish salad, add ¾ pounds coarsely chopped medium shrimp or ¾ pounds shredded cooked chicken.

U.S.A. Rice Council
Houston, TX

HARBOR FESTIVAL

MORRO BAY

Annual. First weekend in October.

If the old adage, "you are what you eat" is true, you'll be sweet, rich, spicy, and deliciously delectable after you've tasted the satisfying seafood delicacies served during the Morro Bay Harbor Festival. In a dramatic waterfront setting, this event celebrates one of California's few honest-to-goodness fishing villages.

The festival showcases seafood, the commercial fishing industry, and the diversity of the central coast's marine life and coastal lifestyles. In recognition of October as National Seafood Month, the festival's California Seafood Fair, sponsored by the California Seafood Council, features a menu of California-caught marine cuisine. Complementing the sea fare is a selection of varietals from the area's finest vintners, as well as a premium beer-tasting opportunity.

Whatever you do, plan plenty of time to visit the festival's more than two hundred exhibits, including a Maritime Heritage Pavilion, Marine & Watersports Expo, and the Port o' Call Expo of commercial exhibitors. The tiny tykes will soon discover there's a harbor full of fun, excitement, and entertainment at Kids' Cove. Everyone has the opportunity to tour a variety of fishing boats, talk one-to-one with the commercial fishermen, and see fresh fish displayed.

If you love to shop, there's plenty for sale by Harborfest arts and crafts vendors. You'll find boating togs, nautical art, sculpture and decorator items, boating accessories, hammocks, and plenty of fresh fish to take home with you.

(Continued)

While you're here, catch the musical entertainment. Seven stages of talented live performers entertain with jazz, big band, country, blues, rock, and, of course, sea chanteys. From dockside to deep sea, this festival makes a splash with major attractions as diverse as the commercial fishermens' Albacore & More Barbecue, ship tours, a 35-ton sand sculpture created by the world champion sandscape crew, plus environmental, marine life, and California casual lifestyle displays.

SHRIMP IN RIESLING/DIJON SAUCE

In a large heavy skillet, heat oil and butter until a haze forms. Add garlic and wine and bring to a simmer. Whisk in mustard. Add shrimp and cook until shrimp are pink (3 to 4 minutes). Serve with sourdough bread for dipping.

Patricia Ballard, author
Fine Wine in Food and Wine in Everyday Cooking
Paso Robles, CA

3 tablespoons olive oil

3 tablespoons butter

4 large cloves garlic, minced

1 cup Bonny Doon Vineyard Pacific Rim Riesling

2 tablespoons Dijon mustard

2 pounds shrimp, shelled and deveined

FRESH THRASHER SHARK WITH CHIPOTLE CHILI, CILANTRO, AND LIME SAUCE

Sauce

1 chipotle chili, chopped

1 teaspoon adobo sauce

1 cup sour cream

1 cup plain yogurt

1 cup mayonnaise

1 small bunch cilantro, chopped

juice of 3 limes

shark fillets

teriyaki sauce

olive oil

clarified margarine

Combine sauce ingredients in food processor and purée. Marinate shark fillets in teriyaki sauce. Grill or sauté in olive oil and clarified margarine. Top fillets with puréed sauce and serve with a loaf of good homemade bread. Makes enough sauce for approximately 12 shark fillets.

The Sow's Ear (bistro)
Cambria, CA

ROBIN'S SALMON BISQUE

Melt butter in a large pot. Add leeks, mushrooms, and garlic. Sauté for approximately 5 minutes. Add the clam juice, tomatoes, parsley, dill, salt, and pepper. Heat this broth to almost boiling and add salmon. Cook the salmon approximately 3 to 5 minutes. Then add cream and whisk in flour. Bring to heat and serve. Garnish with fresh dill sprigs.

Chef Robin and Shanny Covey
Robin's (restaurant)
Cambria, CA

1 cube butter

2 large leeks, sliced

1/2 pound mushrooms

1 tablespoon crushed garlic

46-ounce can clam juice

4 cups crushed tomatoes

1/2 cup chopped parsley

2 teaspoons dill weed

1 teaspoon salt

1/2 teaspoon pepper

4 cups salmon, deboned and cut into 1/2-inch cubes

4 cups cream

1/2 cup flour

HARVEST FESTIVAL

ARROYO GRANDE

Annual. Last weekend in September.

19

Arroyo Grande's Harvest Festival has been going strong since it originated in 1937. Each year as the area's smorgasbord of agricultural crops begins to be harvested, the residents of this central coast community welcome the arrival of the local vegetable harvest by indulging in a weekend of celebration and excitement. This downtown celebration typically includes a wonderful hometown parade featuring antique and classic cars, floats, bands, and plenty of dazzling fun.

Free entertainment, good food, and a great time is what the Harvest Festival is all about. You'll enjoy some of Mother Nature's most delicious gifts as you see and sample innovative dishes filled with lettuce, snow peas, red and green peppers, strawberries, broccoli, carrots, cauliflower, zucchini, and celery from local growing fields.

In addition to the Harvest Festival, Arroyo Grande's annual Strawberry Festival is traditionally held over the three-day Memorial Day weekend. Events include two days of arts and crafts, games for children, minstrels, mimes, jugglers, and a whole lot of locally grown strawberries.

Driving along California's scenic U.S. Highway 101, you might very well think there's no reason to pull off and take a peek at this small town's old-fashioned charm and hospitality. But if you don't, you're missing out on some remarkable travel experiences.

BROCCOLI SALAD

Mix salad ingredients; set aside. Mix dressing ingredients, pour over salad $^1/_2$ hour before serving.

Heather Jensen
Arroyo Grande, CA

Salad

1 to 2 bunches broccoli, flowerets only

$^1/_2$ large red onion, sliced thin

8 ounces mushrooms, sliced

$^1/_2$ pound bacon, cooked, crumbled

$^1/_2$ cup salted sunflower seeds

Dressing

1 cup mayonnaise

$^1/_2$ cup sugar

$^1/_4$ cup red wine vinegar

CAULIFLOWER SALAD

Salad

4 cups cauliflower flowerets

1/2 cup chopped onion

1/2 cup pimento

salt and pepper to taste

1 cup chopped ripe olives

2/3 cup chopped green pepper

crisp salad greens

Dressing

1/2 cup salad oil

3 tablespoons lemon juice

1 teaspoon sugar

2 teaspoons salt

Line bowl with greens. Mix and add all other ingredients. Refrigerate 4 hours before serving.

John Looney, publisher
Family Travel Log (newspaper)
Kewanee, IL

PEA AND SHRIMP SALAD

Bring shelled peas to a boil and cook al dente, about 4 to 5 minutes. In a large bowl, combine all ingredients and mix gently. Refrigerate for at least 4 hours before serving.

Jane Donati
Arroyo Grande, CA

- 1 pound shelled peas
- 3/4 to 1 pound small shrimp
- 1/2 cup diced green onions
- 1/2 cup diced celery
- 1/2 cup slivered almonds
- 1 to 2 teaspoons Worcestershire sauce
- salt and pepper to taste
- 1/2 cup mayonnaise
- juice of 1 lemon

ZUCCHINI PANCAKES

4 medium zucchini, coarsely grated

½ onion, chopped
(sweet variety, if available)

1 clove garlic, chopped

2 eggs, beaten

2 teaspoons flour

a pinch or two of chopped parsley

2 tablespoons grated
Parmesan cheese

5 teaspoons olive oil

Pat the grated zucchini with paper towels to dry, gently press excess moisture out. In mixing bowl, combine well all ingredients except oil. Heat oil in skillet; drop batter into hot oil with large serving spoon. Flatten with spatula. Fry until golden brown on both sides. As each batch is cooked, hold in warm oven on plate lined with paper toweling.

Mildred Howie
Healdsburg, CA

HOLLYWOOD BOWL SUMMER FESTIVAL

LOS ANGELES/HOLLYWOOD

Annual. June-September.

20

Los Angeles is so large it's almost impossible to know where it begins or ends. Without a doubt, two of the city's most popular visitor destinations are Hollywood and the Hollywood Bowl. Built in 1929, the famous Hollywood Bowl has hosted internationally known musicians, performers, presidents, Easter sunrise services, the Los Angeles Philharmonic, and the Hollywood Bowl Orchestra.

A rhapsody of musical entertainments fills the Hollywood Bowl year-round, but the glittering opening of the Hollywood Bowl Summer Festival signals the beginning of the Los Angeles/Hollywood summer season. The outdoor amphitheater seats nearly 1,800 people, so anticipate some lines. The Bowl encourages packing a picnic dinner; arriving early; enjoying people watching, feasting, and avoiding the crowds that invade the place close to performance time.

You can buy food at on-site restaurants or order picnic baskets from delicatessens, but it's more fun to take your own. Hundreds of jovial patrons bring candles, candlesticks, champagne, wine, and set up some very elaborate dining. Others bring coolers, cold sandwiches, plastic utensils, and paper plates. It doesn't matter. The point is to feast on flavorful concoctions, relax, enjoy the crowd, and absorb some fine entertainment performed under the stars.

A portable picnic doesn't have to mean a lot of work. To prove the point, the following menu and recipes were created especially for a Hollywood Bowl Summer Festival picnic by Gail Hobbs, author, food consultant, and culinary expert.

MENU FOR YOUR BOWL PICNIC (recipes follow)

- Cajun Crab Quiche
- Salad with Creamy Buttermilk Dressing
- Strawberries and Cream
- Champagne or White Wine

CAJUN CRAB QUICHE

1 tablespoon butter

1 tablespoon dry sherry

1/2 cup diced onion

1/2 cup grated carrot

1/2 cup chopped mushrooms

3 eggs

8 ounces heavy whipping cream

10 drops hot pepper sauce

1/4 to 1/2 teaspoon Cajun spice

2 tablespoons dry sherry

1 cup grated Swiss cheese

2 6-ounce cans crabmeat

salt and white pepper to taste

single pie crust, lightly baked

paprika

Preheat oven to 400°. Melt butter in a skillet over medium heat, add sherry, onion, carrot, and mushrooms. Sauté for about 5 minutes, until onion is translucent and carrot is softened. In a large bowl, beat eggs until well combined. Pour in cream and continue to beat for another minute. Stir in hot pepper sauce, Cajun spice, sherry, cheese, crab, and sautéed vegetables. Season with salt and pepper to taste. Pour into pie crust. Sprinkle with paprika. Place in center of oven and bake for 35 minutes or until center is slightly firm to the touch. Do not overcook. Remove from oven and allow to set for 10 or 15 minutes. Serve warm or at room temperature.

CREAMY BUTTERMILK DRESSING

Whisk all ingredients together very well. Flavor improves overnight. Keep well chilled. Serve over a crisp salad made of red or green leaf lettuce, thinly sliced red pepper, and Bermuda onion.

1 cup buttermilk

1 cup mayonnaise

1/2 cup grated Romano or Parmesan cheese

1 teaspoon granulated garlic

1/2 teaspoon salt

1/2 teaspoon white pepper

STRAWBERRIES & CREAM

1 pint fresh ripe strawberries, hulled, washed, and dried

granulated sugar to taste

sour cream

Lightly sprinkle berries with sugar. Keep cool. When ready to serve, top with a dollop of sour cream.

HUCK FINN JUBILEE

VICTORVILLE

Annual. Father's Day weekend.

In the Samuel Clemens classic, *The Adventures of Huckleberry Finn*, Huck can be heard saying, "I catched a catfish and haggled him open with my saw, and towards sundown I started my camp-fire and had supper. Then I set out a line to catch some fish for breakfast." The Huck Finn Jubilee offers you and your family a chance to relive the adventures of this fictional character.

This turn-of-the-century river festival comes complete with catfishing, raft building, big top circus, handmade crafts, and woodchip barbecues. The festival honors Huck Finn and Tom Sawyer. In addition, there are more than 30 hours of country and bluegrass music. All of the events take place at Mojave Narrows Regional Park.

The music is performed outdoors in the park's large, grassy meadow. All you need to settle back and enjoy the really topnotch entertainment is to bring your own camp chair to sit on and a cooler full of sarsaparilla or other libation.

There's so much to do, you'll probably not be able to enjoy it all. Hayrides, egg tossin', and raft building are among the many activities. There are clogging and country boot-stompin' exhibitions and contests. This is a rare, old-fashioned event that's perfect for the entire family.

Vittles, crafts, and mountain men are seen everywhere throughout all three days of the event. Bring your pole and license and join dozens of Huck Finn look-alikes as they compete for award-winning catfish. You may get a winning catfish to take your line.

Victorville is situated approximately 95 miles northeast of Los Angeles, off Interstate 15 at the edge of the Mojave Desert.

QUICKLY SAUTÉED CATFISH FILLETS

2 Sunkist lemons, cut into 12 wedges

1 pound catfish fillets, cut into 4 serving-size pieces

2 tablespoons flour

1/4 teaspoon paprika

1 tablespoon olive or salad oil

salt and pepper to taste

Squeeze juice of 2 lemon wedges over both sides of fish fillets. Let stand 5 minutes. Lightly pat dry with paper toweling. Combine flour and paprika on a plate. Dip fish fillets in flour to coat lightly. Heat oil and sauté fish over medium-high heat for 3 to 4 minutes on each side, or until fish is opaque and flakes easily with a fork. Salt and pepper to taste. Garnish each serving with remaining lemon wedges.

Sunkist Growers, Inc.
Van Nuys, CA

Orange roughy, red snapper, or halibut may be substituted for catfish in this recipe.

CORN SPOON BREAD

Pour the corn (including liquid), milk, and cornmeal into a bowl, mix. Beat egg yolks until creamed, add to mixture. Beat egg whites. Just before they are stiff, add to the mixture and stir well. Salt and pepper to taste. Bake in hot oven until top is golden brown. Can be eaten with a spoon or sliced.

Edna McMahan, contributor
Recipes from Across the United States
Kewanee, IL

1 2-pound can whole kernel corn
2 cups milk
1 cup cornmeal
3 eggs, separated
salt and pepper

CORN MEAL GRIDDLE CAKES

1 cup sifted flour

$^1/_2$ cup cornmeal

$^1/_2$ teaspoon salt

$^1/_2$ teaspoon baking soda

1 teaspoon sugar

1 egg

1 cup sour milk

$^1/_2$ cup boiling water

3 tablespoons shortening, melted

Sift dry ingredients 3 times. Beat egg, milk, boiling water, and shortening together. Add to dry ingredients, stirring constantly to keep smooth. Drop batter on hot griddle, lower heat. Cook until top is full of tiny bubbles, turn and brown other side. Serve hot with syrup.

Terry Poland
Oxnard, CA

FARM-RAISED CATFISH WITH TANGY ORANGE AND LEMON SAUCE

To make the sauce, combine orange juice, vegetable oil, soy sauce, pepper, lemon juice, and garlic in a bowl. Brush catfish fillets with sauce mixture. Place fish on lightly oiled grill (4 inches above hot coals). Grill for 5 minutes, brushing frequently with sauce. Turn and grill for 5 minutes longer or until fish flakes easily when tested with a fork. This recipe is excellent when broiled, as well.

National Fisheries Institute
Arlington, VA

Sauce

1/4 cup orange juice

2 tablespoons vegetable oil

2 tablespoons light soy sauce

1/8 teaspoon pepper

1 tablespoon lemon juice

1 clove garlic, minced

2 pounds farm-raised catfish fillets

INTERNATIONAL TAMALE FESTIVAL

INDIO

Annual. First weekend in December.

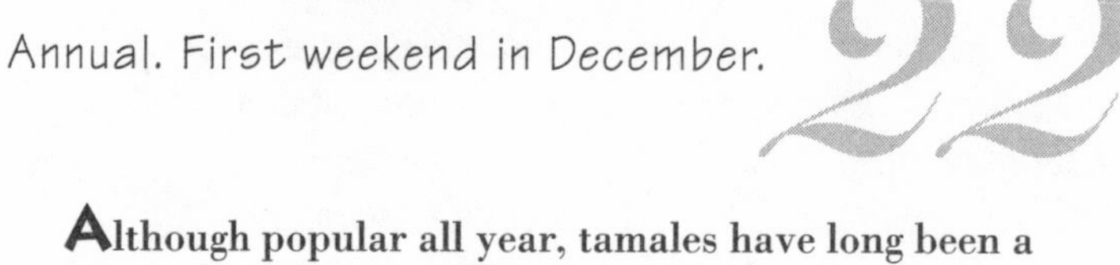

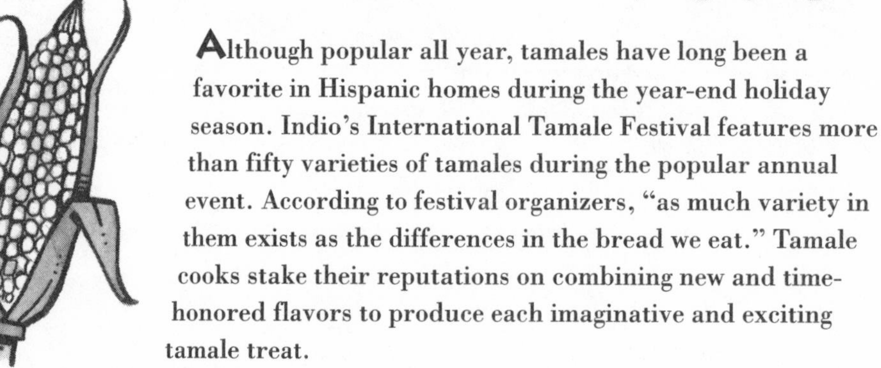

Although popular all year, tamales have long been a favorite in Hispanic homes during the year-end holiday season. Indio's International Tamale Festival features more than fifty varieties of tamales during the popular annual event. According to festival organizers, "as much variety in them exists as the differences in the bread we eat." Tamale cooks stake their reputations on combining new and time-honored flavors to produce each imaginative and exciting tamale treat.

The minute you arrive in the Coachella Valley community of Indio, you'll discover the Old Town streets have been transformed into a festive collage of color, art, music, and (of course) tamales. You'll move to the sounds of marching bands and international recording stars. You'll clap to the music of mariachi music and sway in time with the folk dancers. Throughout this two-day celebration, the festival air is filled with musical sounds and dancing feet.

The event's Tamale Festival Parade begins promptly at 10 A.M. Saturday when more than one hundred entrants make their way through the downtown streets. Participants include colorfully costumed marching bands, drill teams, and dance groups. Others adding gusto to the procession are lavish floats, spit-and-polished vintage automobiles, and the spirited Marine Corps Marching Band.

Following the parade, everyone gathers at the festival grounds to mingle with the dozens of tamale vendors, artists, and craftspeople. Children love visiting the petting zoo and bounce booth. Hometown events include a carnival, pony rides, game booths, and entertainment on two stages.

The star of the festival, naturally, is the tamale. You'll discover such diverse creations as tiger shrimp and pineapple tamales along with the ones filled with traditional pork, beef, and chicken loved by the people of Latin America.

The International Tamale Festival takes place on the Old Town streets of Miles Avenue and Smurr and Towne streets. From Interstate 10, exit at Jackson Street and proceed south. Indio is located two hours east of Los Angeles and Orange County and two and one-half hours from San Diego.

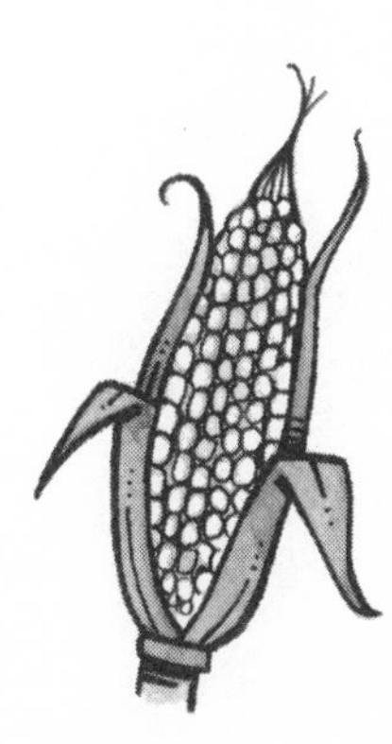

SENIOR CENTER TAMALES

1/2 pound dried husks (for approximately 50 tamales).

Masa

1 1/2 cups lard

4 cups masa flour

3 teaspoons salt

2 3/4 cups water (or use pork, beef, or chicken broth from cooking meat for the filling recipe)

Filling

1 medium-size onion, chopped

1 1/2 tablespoons lard

2 cups finely diced or shredded, cooked pork, chicken, or turkey

1 small can jalapeño chilies

1 cup Mexican red chili sauce or enchilada sauce

1 cup pitted olives

Soak dried husks in warm water. Mix lard until fluffy, blend in masa flour, salt, and warm water until dough holds together. Cover with damp cloth and keep cool until ready to use. Makes enough for about 50 tamales.

In a frying pan, cook onion in lard until soft. Stir in meat, chilies, and chili sauce. Simmer uncovered for 10 minutes, stirring to blend flavors. Makes 2 1/2 to 3 cups of filling.

Spread 2 tablespoons masa dough on husk in a rectangle about 5x4-inch. If husk is not wide enough, use some masa dough to paste another piece of husk onto the back of the first husk. Spoon 2 tablespoons meat filling into the center of the masa and insert an olive. Fold right side over to center, then fold left side over filling. Fold up bottom end over mound of dough. When tamales are folded, place them in tamale kettle or on a rack placed 1 inch above boiling water in a covered container. Stack tamales on rack standing up, folded side down. Stack loosely so that steam can cook tamales evenly, 45 minutes to an hour. When masa is firm and doesn't stick to shuck, the tamales are done.

Indio Senior Center
Indio, CA

Masa, the dough for tamales, is available at Mexican markets and some supermarkets. The best masa of all is homemade, and good tamale makers proudly develop and serve their own specialties.

TAMALE WITH GOAT CHEESE, SUN-DRIED TOMATO, AND PECANS

Prepare masa in a mixing bowl with paddle attachment. Add the vegetable shortening and mix until soft and creamy (the time depends on how cold the shortening is). Blend in warm water, masa flour, salt, and baking powder. Mix well for at least 5 to 8 minutes on medium speed, until light and fluffy and the dough holds together. Transfer to another bowl and keep refrigerated.

In the mixing bowl, place the goat cheese, black pepper, and oregano. Mix well with the paddle attachment and slowly add the chopped pecans and sun-dried tomato.

Assemble tamales in husk, using 3 ounces of masa and 2 ounces of filling for a 5-ounce tamale, or 1½ ounces of masa and 1 ounce of filling for a 2½-ounce tamale. Steam for 45 minutes. Makes about 35 tamales.

International Tamale Festival
Indio, CA

¾ pound 100% vegetable shortening

8 ounces warm water

5 pounds masa flour

¾ ounce salt

1 ounce baking powder

3¼ pounds goat cheese

½ teaspoon ground black pepper

1 tablespoon dry Greek oregano

4 ounces chopped pecans

2 ounces sun-dried tomato soaked in hot water

½ pound dried husks, soaked in water

MOM'S CALIFORNIA TAMALE PIE

1 pound lean ground beef

3/4 cup yellow cornmeal

1 1/2 cups milk

1 egg, beaten

1 package chili seasoning mix

1 teaspoon seasoned salt

16-ounce can tomatoes, cut up

2 cups whole kernel corn, drained

3 ounces sliced ripe olives

1 cup grated cheddar cheese

In skillet, cook meat until crumbly; drain. In a large mixing bowl, combine and mix corn meal, milk, and egg. Add meat, chili seasoning mix, seasoned salt, tomatoes, corn, and olives. Put mixture into a lightly greased or sprayed casserole, cover, and cook approximately 1 hour at 350°. Sprinkle cheese over the top, cook approximately 5 minutes or until cheese melts.

Bob Carter
Oxnard, CA

Although no substitute for fresh, homemade tamales, this simple recipe may satisfy your tamale-taste longings between trips to the International Tamale Festival for the real thing. The recipe is one my mom used to make.

OLIVE TURKEY TAMALE BAKE

4 ears corn with husks

1 pound ground turkey

2 tablespoons vegetable oil

1 cup California ripe olive wedges

$^1/_2$ cup chopped green onion, half green, half bulb

1 tablespoon chili powder

$1^1/_2$ cups grated pepper jack or Monterey Jack cheese

Husk corn, tearing husk as little as possible. Save outer husks, cleaning off the silk. Drop corn and saved husks into large pot of boiling water. Return to boil and simmer for 5 minutes. Drain through colander.

Meanwhile, sauté turkey in oil in skillet over high heat until browned. Using large knife, quickly slice corn kernels from cob and add olives, onion, and chili powder to turkey. Sauté 2 minutes longer. Remove from heat and stir in cheese. Line bottom of $1^1/_2$-quart casserole with half the softened husks. Turn turkey filling over husks and make a layer of remaining husks on top, tucking in at edges. Cover and bake at 425°for 20 minutes or until hot in center.

California Olive Industry
Fresno, CA

LEMON FESTIVAL

GOLETA

Annual. Second Sunday in October.

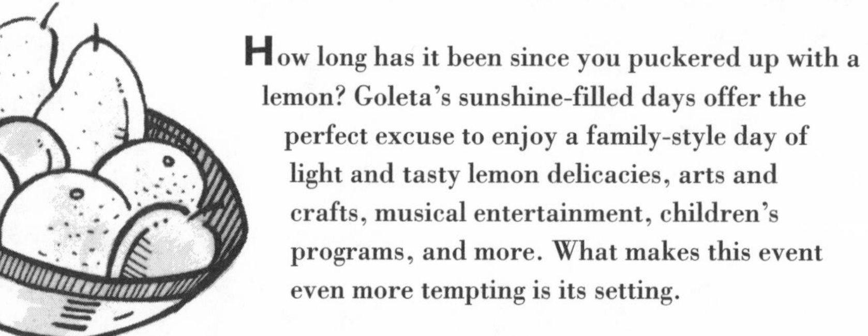

How long has it been since you puckered up with a lemon? Goleta's sunshine-filled days offer the perfect excuse to enjoy a family-style day of light and tasty lemon delicacies, arts and crafts, musical entertainment, children's programs, and more. What makes this event even more tempting is its setting.

Held on the grounds of the historic, Victorian-style Stowe House and the South Coast Railroad Museum, the festival offers a chance to get a good look into California's past. The museum exhibits working railroad equipment, artifacts, photographs, and memorabilia. Here's a chance to get that railroad engineer's hat you've always wanted. If you're a kid (or feel like one), try taking the miniature train ride.

Local residents cook up some of the best-tasting lemon concoctions around. Of course there's a lemon pie contest, but the fun doesn't stop there. Lemon growers offer educational and informative exhibits and displays, you can ride tall and proud on a fire engine and train, and learn about history on a tour of the fascinating Stowe House. The home's outbuildings hold antique farm equipment, a working blacksmith shop, and a bunkhouse. It's like walking back in time.

Treat the little tykes to face painting, a petting zoo, pony rides, and games. Jugglers, clowns, and musicians fill the air with laughter and music.

Parking is limited at the event site, but free shuttle service is provided nearby. You'll have a better time, and arrive at the festival more relaxed, if you park your car and take the shuttle.

Santa Barbara and Goleta tend to flow together. Each city is easily reached by U.S. Highway 101. In a town sometimes overlooked by travelers, you'll experience a feeling of small-town enthusiasm and pride.

All recipes for this section supplied by Sunkist Growers, Inc., Van Nuys, CA.

EASIEST-EVER FISH STEAKS IN FOIL

1 pound salmon, halibut, swordfish, or shark steaks (1 inch thick)

grated peel and juice of ½ Sunkist lemon

paprika and/or salt, or seafood herb blend, or Cajun seasoning, or dried or chopped fresh dill

½ tablespoon butter or margarine

Spray 18-inch square of heavy-duty aluminum foil with non-stick cooking spray. Arrange fish steaks in center of foil. Sprinkle with lemon juice, then grated peel. Lightly sprinkle with one seasoning or herb; dot with butter. Bring two sides of foil together above fish; fold down several times to secure. Fold in short ends of foil to secure. Place on baking sheet. Bake at 450°for 11 to 12 minutes, or until fish is opaque and flakes easily with a fork. Remove from foil and spoon drippings over fish. Serve with lemon wedges, if desired.

SEASONED LEMON BUTTER PATTIES

In a small bowl, combine all ingredients. On wax paper, shape butter mixture into 7x1-inch roll or rectangle. Roll up tightly in the wax paper; chill. Slice into patties. Serve 1 to 2 patties on grilled, broiled, or poached fish steaks or fillets. Good on pasta, too. Makes about $^1/_2$ cup.

Try substituting 1 to 2 teaspoons of 1 of the following finely chopped herbs for parsley: basil, dill, marjoram, mint, or tarragon.

- $^1/_2$ cup butter or margarine, softened
- grated peel and juice of $^1/_2$ Sunkist lemon
- 1 tablespoon finely chopped green onion
- 1 tablespoon finely chopped fresh parsley
- $^1/_4$ teaspoon seasoned salt
- $^1/_8$ teaspoon white pepper

LIGHT AND LEMONY DILL SPREAD

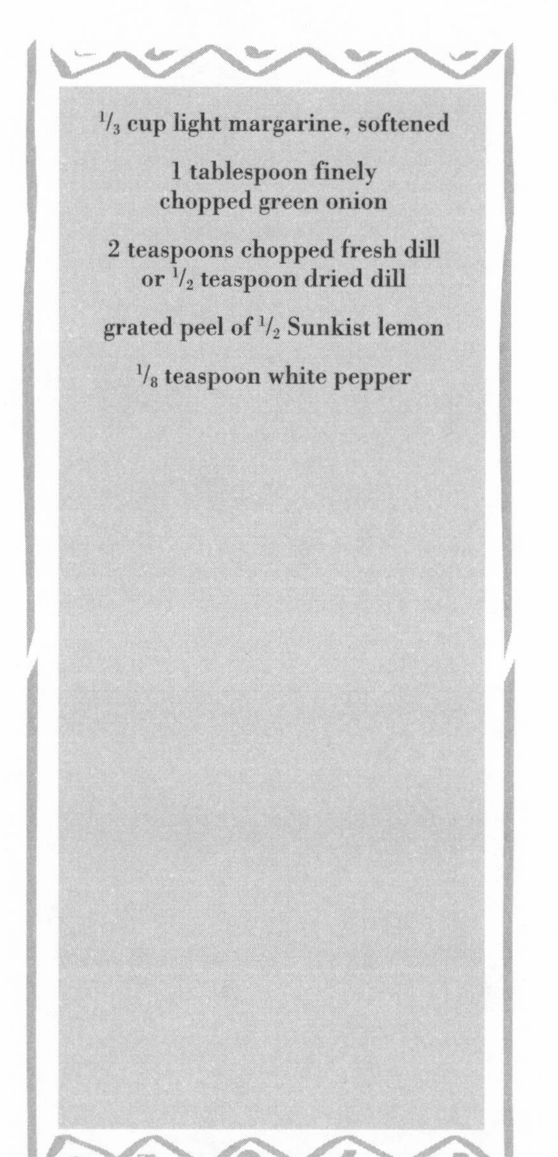

1/3 cup light margarine, softened

1 tablespoon finely chopped green onion

2 teaspoons chopped fresh dill or 1/2 teaspoon dried dill

grated peel of 1/2 Sunkist lemon

1/8 teaspoon white pepper

In a small bowl, combine all ingredients. Serve 1 to 2 teaspoons over each serving of grilled, broiled, or poached fish steaks or fillets. Makes about 1/3 cup.

CARIBBEAN SALSA

In bowl, sprinkle lemon peel and juice over avocado. Add remaining ingredients and gently stir. Serve at room temperature, or cover and chill 1 to 2 hours. Serve with baked or roasted chicken.

grated peel of 1/2 Sunkist lemon

juice of 1 Sunkist lemon (3 tablespoons)

1 medium avocado, peeled, pitted, finely chopped

1 papaya or mango, peeled, seeded, finely chopped

1/3 cup diced purple or white onion

1 tablespoon honey

1/2 to 1 small jalapeño pepper, minced (optional)

generous dash each cinnamon and allspice

LOBSTER FESTIVAL

Redondo Beach

Annual. Third weekend in October.

I bet you thought all the great lobster festivals were in New England. Right?

The Redondo Lobster Festival is your chance to enjoy one of California's favorite coastal feastings. The festival, although a fledgling celebration honoring the great crustaceans, is already a highlight among California's many food-oriented celebrations.

There's always something new going on, but you're always guaranteed some great feasting. The festival brings in at least 5,000 lobsters from Maine and California. How's this for fresh lobster: you can snorkel in Seaside Lagoon, catch your own California lobster, and have it cooked to order. Throughout the event, other food vendors offer seafood-laden items such as fish tacos, as well as chicken, barbecue ribs, sausages, gourmet tamales, and desserts.

The festival focuses on kids, and Camp Crustacean is a special area at the event site with rides and games aimed at the younger generation. The California State Chowder Championship gives two awards. The People's Choice goes to the best chowder served at the event as voted by attendees, and the Judge's Choice goes to the chowder selected best by a panel of VIP judges.

Wait! There's more. Los Angeles County lifeguards hold squid races, and sculptors create giant sand lobsters. The musical menu features a full line-up of music and entertainment, including the mellow sounds of jazz and steel bands.

LOBSTER SAUCE WITH LINGUINE

Steam lobsters in 1 inch of water for 8 to 10 minutes. Remove and let cool. Reserve 1/4 cup of liquid (lobster broth). After lobsters cool, pick meat out of the shell and cut into large pieces. Carefully extract claw meat and leave whole.

In a large skillet, sauté garlic and onions in butter for 5 to 8 minutes, until onions are soft. Do not allow to brown. Add mushrooms and cook water out of them, then remove mushrooms and reserve. Add wine and reduce by one-half. Add tomatoes and cook 2 to 3 minutes. Cook linguine.

Add lobster broth and yogurt, reduce by one-fourth. Bring to a boil, simmer, add lobster, scallions, parsley, reserved mushrooms, and seasoning. Add Parmesan cheese to thicken. Toss half of sauce with cooked linguine. Arrange on plate, pour remaining half of sauce over each serving. Top with the whole claw meat.

National Fisheries Institute
Arlington, VA

3 1/4 pounds total live Maine lobsters (serves 6)

2 cloves garlic, minced

1 1/2 cups sliced onion

2 tablespoons butter

1/2 cup sliced mushrooms

1/4 cup white wine

2 cups fresh tomatoes, peeled, seeded, diced

1 pound linguine

1/4 cup plain yogurt

1/2 cup scallions, in 1/2-inch pieces

2 tablespoons chopped parsley

Old Bay or seafood seasoning, to taste

1/2 cup grated Parmesan cheese

SEAFOOD STEW

meat from 2 small lobsters, chopped

1/8 cup olive oil

3 large tomatoes, chopped

1 1/2 cups tomato juice

2 cups dry white wine

3 cups fish stock

3 cloves garlic, chopped

1/2 cup finely chopped fresh parsley

2 bay leaves

2 dozen clams, steamed and shucked

2 dozen shrimp, shelled

Sauté lobster gently in oil for 2 minutes. Add tomatoes and juice. Cook for a few minutes, then add all other ingredients and simmer for 20 minutes. This is great served with crusty bread.

Maine Windjammers Association

The good folks at the Maine Windjammers Association sent me this delicious recipe used aboard the ship *J & E Riggin*. The vessel was built in 1927 and is listed as a National Historic Landmark.

LOBSTER CACCIATORE WITH LINGUINE

2 pounds lobster

1/4 cup olive oil

1 cup finely chopped onion

1 small green pepper, seeded, cut into thin strips

1 clove garlic, finely chopped

1/2 teaspoon dried oregano

1 tablespoon freshly chopped basil (optional)

1/2 teaspoon salt or more to taste

fresh ground pepper to taste

1 dried hot pepper, crumbled, or 1/4 teaspoon hot pepper flakes

1 1/2 cups canned plum tomatoes, partially drained and crushed

1/4 cup dry red wine

1/2 pound freshly cooked linguine

If the lobster has not been dressed, do so. Cut the lobster into bite-size pieces.

Heat the oil in a large, heavy skillet, add the lobster, and cook over moderate heat for 3 to 4 minutes. The lobster will give off some liquid. Add the onion, green pepper, garlic, oregano, basil, salt, pepper, and hot pepper; cook for an additional 3 to 4 minutes. Add the tomatoes and wine, bring to a boil, cover, lower heat, and simmer for 10 minutes. Do not overcook. Correct the seasoning.

Serve with freshly cooked, well-drained linguine. Grind more black pepper over the top just before serving.

Maine Lobster Promotion Council
Bangor, ME

LOBSTER PUFFS

½ fresh lobster

2 cups flour

½ teaspoon salt

several dashes cayenne pepper

3 teaspoons baking powder

1 egg, well beaten

1 cup milk

2 cups peanut oil for frying

Pick over the lobster meat, if necessary, then chop it up. In a large mixing bowl, sift together flour, salt, cayenne pepper, and baking powder. In another bowl, blend together the egg and milk, stir in the lobster meat; add this to the flour mixture and mix well.

Heat the oil in a large skillet until hot but not smoking, or in an electric fryer set at 365°. Drop the lobster mixture by rounded tablespoonfuls into the hot oil, fry 3 minutes or until golden. Don't crowd the pan. Drain on paper towels, keep warm until all are done. Serve piping hot as an appetizer or a first course with tartar sauce.

Maine Lobster Promotion Council
Bangor, ME

MEXICAN FIESTA & MARIACHI MUSIC FESTIVAL

OJAI

Annual. September date varies.

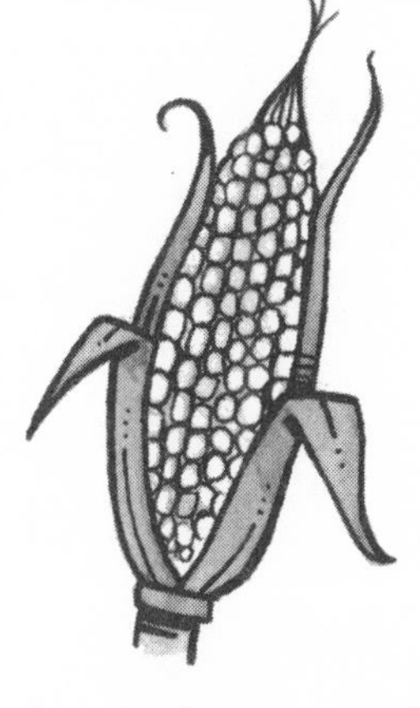

Hungry for real Mexican flavor?

For more than 30 years people have delighted in experiencing the blending of ethnic food, cultural exhibits, lively entertainment, and Latino-inspired arts during the Mexican Fiesta & Mariachi Music Festival. Now it's your turn to pack up the car, take a ride, and participate.

The expansive food offerings cook up some tantalizing tastes of Mexico and the United States. In addition to traditional dishes such as Pico de Gallo, Chilaquiles, and Horchata, there's always something new and tasty making its entry onto the festival food menu. You'll find fiery chilies, savory salsas, and flavorful flan to tempt your taste buds.

The State of Jalisco in Mexico is the home of mariachi music. During the fiesta you'll be tapping your feet to the sounds of several mariachi groups. Most of the ensembles are composed of violins, trumpets, vihuela, guitars, and guitarron.

In addition to observing some fine footwork by festival dancers, you might find yourself invited to join in the fun as folk dancers perform dances from various regions of Mexico. The regions represented include Veracruz, Michoacan, El Norte, and Jalisco. You'll discover that each region has its own style of dance movements and dress. Always a favorite, the Ballet Folklorico performs its special blend of colorful music, dance, and clothing.

Held in Libby Park, in the center of downtown Ojai, the annual event is dedicated to the educational development of youth of Mexican heritage.

HORCHATA

6 tablespoons uncooked rice

1/4 cup water

6 ounces blanched almonds

1 1-inch long cinnamon stick

3 2-inch strips of lime zest

2 1/4 cups hot water

4 cups water

1 cup sugar

Pulverize the rice in a blender with water. Transfer to medium mixing bowl and add almonds, cinnamon stick, and lime zest. Stir in 2 1/4 cups of hot tap water. Cover and let stand for at least 6 hours. Scoop mixture into blender and blend for 3 to 4 minutes or until smooth. Add 2 cups of water and blend a few seconds more. Place large sieve over mixing bowl and line with 3 layers of cheesecloth. Pour the almond-rice mixture slowly into the bowl. Squeeze cheesecloth to expel all remaining liquids. Finish the Horchata by adding 2 cups of water and stirring in enough sugar to sweeten to your taste. Cover and refrigerate. Stir before serving.

Mexican Fiesta & Mariachi Music Festival
Ojai, CA

GUACAMOLE PICADO

Mix onion, chilies, garlic, and coriander in mixing bowl. Add avocado and tomato. Mix, making a thick mass, and flavor with salt. Add a little lime juice to give it zing. Place guacamole in a pottery bowl, sprinkle with chopped onion or crumbled fresh cheese to garnish.

Mexican Fiesta & Mariachi Music Festival
Ojai, CA

To prevent avocado from turning brown, return seed pits to serving bowl until ready to serve.

1/2 small onion, finely chopped

2 serrano chilies, stemmed, seeded, and finely chopped

1 clove garlic, peeled and finely chopped

10 sprigs fresh coriander, chopped

3 ripe avocados, mashed

1 ripe tomato, cored and finely chopped

1/2 teaspoon salt

juice of 1/2 lime

chopped onion or crumbled fresh cheese to garnish

CARNITAS CON SALSA CHILI VERDE

- $2^1/_2$ pounds pork, trimmed
- $^1/_2$ teaspoon salt
- 8 ounces fresh tomatillos, husked and washed
- 2 California or Anaheim chilies, roasted, skin peeled off
- $^1/_2$ cup onion
- $^1/_8$ cup garlic
- 2 serrano chilies, diced
- 6 sprigs cilantro
- $^1/_4$ cup water
- zest of lime
- $^1/_2$ teaspoon salt

Place pork in saucepan with enough water to cover. Add $^1/_2$ teaspoon salt. Simmer covered for 40 minutes, turning occasionally. Uncover, boil away water until pork is frying in its own lard. Allow to fry for 30 minutes. Remove and drain on paper towel.

Boil tomatillos in salted water to taste for 10 minutes, then drain. Boil Anaheim chilies. Place tomatillos and boiled chilies in blender with onions, garlic, diced serrano chilies, and cilantro. Blend until puréed.

Place purée in sauce dish and thin to a medium-thick consistency with $^1/_4$ cup water. Stir in lime zest. Add purée to fried pork pieces and gently warm over low heat. Stir and salt to taste.

This dish may be eaten as a stew or rolled in flour tortillas to make a Chile Verde burrito.

Mexican Fiesta & Mariachi Music Festival
Ojai, CA

BORDER BEEF AND RICE BAKE

2 4.4- to 6.8-ounce packages Spanish seasoned rice mix

1 pound ground beef

1 medium onion, chopped

1 $1^1/_4$-ounce packet taco seasoning mix

6 corn tortillas

2 $14^1/_2$-ounce cans Mexican-style stewed tomatoes*

2 cups shredded Mexican-style cheese blend**

chopped fresh cilantro

Prepare rice according to package directions. Heat large skillet over medium-high heat until hot. Add beef, onion, and seasoning mix. Cook 5 to 7 minutes, or until beef is brown and onion is tender. Remove from heat, drain fat.

Tear three corn tortillas into bite-size pieces and place on bottom of a non-metallic 13x9x2-inch dish. Add half of beef mixture, spreading evenly. Top with half of rice mixture, half of the tomatoes, and half of the cheese. Repeat layers, except cheese. Cover and bake in 400° oven for 15 minutes. Uncover, top with remaining cheese, and bake 10 minutes more or until cheese is melted. Garnish with cilantro.

U.S.A. Rice Council
Houston, TX

*Substitute 2 $14^1/_2$-ounce cans stewed tomatoes plus one 4-ounce can chopped green chillies for Mexican-style, if desired.

**Substitute shredded Monterrey Jack cheese for Mexican-blend, if desired.

NATIONAL DATE FESTIVAL

RIVERSIDE COUNTY

Annual. Mid-February.

26

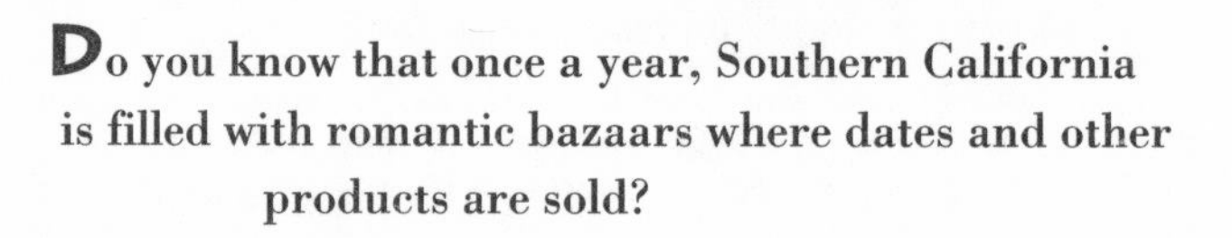

Do you know that once a year, Southern California is filled with romantic bazaars where dates and other products are sold?

Long before Disney brought Aladdin, Ali Baba, and Scheherazade to movie and television screens, the National Date Festival, with its exotic Arabian Nights pageants, has drawn crowds to the desert.

The National Date Festival began in the 1920s as a celebration honoring the end of the date harvest. It became a county fair in 1938 and evolved into the mega-event it is today. More than 95 percent of all dates produced in the United States are harvested on 4,500 acres in the Indio/Coachella Valley area. It's no wonder Indio is considered the date capital of the world.

This is not your ordinary celebration. It's been described as ". . . filled with fantastic family fun." It's all of that and more. In addition to a varied menu of food, libations, and entertainment, the event includes a nightly Arabian Nights Fantasy that's sure to please all members of the family. The pageant is presented on a stage that's an authentic reproduction of a marketplace in ancient Baghdad, where dates, grain, wool, and other products were sold.

Major activities include dozens of date and citrus competitions, date exhibits, date displays, and date shake tastings. After all this, you may want to pick up a copy of Riverside County's *National Date Festival* cookbook, containing award-winning date and citrus recipes. Traditional country fair exhibits highlight fine arts and crafts, livestock, home arts, floriculture, woodworking, and commercial exhibits.

More than half a million people attend the annual Date Festival & County Fair. Reigning over the ten-day extravaganza are Queen Scheherazade and her princesses. The celebration includes dozens of food vendors, camel and ostrich races, colorful costumes, and outdoor bazaars. It's a fitting tribute to the importance of the local date industry.

The National Date Festival is held on the grounds of ExpoCenter, 46350 Arabia Street.

CHICKEN BREASTS COACHELLA

1 cup chopped Sun Giant dates

2 cups seasoned stuffing mix

2/3 cup water

4 tablespoons melted butter or margarine

1 cup chopped celery

6 large chicken breasts, boned

2 tablespoons melted butter or margarine

Sauce

1/2 cup slivered Sun Giant pitted dates

2 tablespoons dry white wine

1 cup orange juice

1/8 teaspoon cinnamon

salt to taste

orange slices for garnish

Mix chopped dates, stuffing mix, water, butter, and celery. Spread on a 12x8-inch greased baking dish or large ovenproof platter. Arrange chicken breasts, skin side up, on top of dressing mixture. Brush with melted butter. Cover with foil and place in 375° oven for 1/2 hour. Remove foil and continue baking until chicken is fork-tender, about 15 to 20 minutes.

In a saucepan, mix slivered dates, wine, orange juice, cinnamon, and salt. Bring to a boil, stirring frequently. Turn down heat and simmer 3 to 4 minutes. Serve sauce hot and on the side as a sauce for chicken breasts. Garnish with orange slices.

National Date Festival cookbook
Indio, CA

PORK LOIN ROAST WITH DATE GLAZE

Place pork loin in shallow roasting pan. Insert meat thermometer in center. Sprinkle with salt and pepper and roast in uncovered 325° oven for 1½ hours.

To prepare date-currant glaze, heat currant jelly over low flame until it liquefies. Add 4 remaining ingredients and cook 3 to 4 minutes, stirring constantly.

Remove meat from oven and baste generously with glaze. Return to the oven and continue roasting for 30 minutes, or until thermometer reaches 180°. Baste occasionally with additional glaze.

National Date Festival
courtesy of "Sun Giant Dates"
Indio, CA

1 boned and rolled pork loin

salt and pepper to taste

1 8-ounce jar red currant jelly

1 cup chopped dates

2 tablespoons wine vinegar

1 teaspoon prepared mustard

½ teaspoon salt

DATE NUT BREAD

8 ounces dates, chopped
1 cup sugar
1 tablespoon butter
1½ cups hot water
2½ cups flour
¼ cup cocoa powder
2 teaspoons baking powder
1 teaspoon salt
1 egg
1 tablespoon vanilla
1½ cups chopped pecans

Place dates, sugar, and butter in a medium bowl and mix in hot water. Allow to sit for approximately 15 minutes, until dates are softened. Meanwhile, combine flour, cocoa, baking powder, and salt, and mix well in a small bowl. When dates are softened, beat in egg and vanilla with a fork. Add dry ingredients to wet mixture and mix well. Stir in pecans. Pour into a greased and floured 9x5-inch loaf pan. Bake in a 350° oven for approximately 60 minutes, or until a toothpick comes out clean.

Gail Hobbs, author
Cookin' in Ventura
Ventura, CA

Do not overbake this tempting bread. After baking, it's best to cool slightly and then remove from pan and finish cooling on a rack.

PALM SPRINGS FRUIT SALAD

2 large oranges

1 pineapple

2 kiwi fruits

4 skinless, boneless chicken breast halves, cooked and cooled

1/2 cup sliced California dates

mint sprigs for garnish

Orange Mint Yogurt Dressing

1 cup plain low-fat yogurt

2 tablespoons honey

2 teaspoons grated orange peel

1 1/2 teaspoons finely chopped candied ginger

1/8 teaspoon salt

1 dash cayenne pepper

1 1/2 teaspoons chopped fresh mint

Remove peel and pith from oranges. Slice into 1/4-inch thick rounds. Quarter and peel pineapple. Slice into 1/2-inch thick slices. Peel kiwi and slice into 1/4-inch thick slices. Arrange oranges, pineapple, and kiwi on 4 salad plates.

Tear chicken into strips. Whisk together all dressing ingredients until well combined. Toss chicken strips with dates and Orange Mint Yogurt Dressing. Divide mixture into 4 portions and arrange evenly on each serving plate. Garnish with mint sprigs.

California Date Administrative Committee
Indio, CA

OBON FESTIVAL

SAN LUIS OBISPO

Annual. Date varies.

27

What a wonderful way to spend a day. The scrumptious smell of teriyaki chicken and rhythmic beat of Taiko drums float through the Obon Festival. Filled with traditional Japanese cultural activities, the event is sponsored by the San Luis Obispo Buddhist Temple.

During the festival hours, you'll find several opportunities to treat your palate to a variety of oriental dishes. Here's your chance to savor the very special flavors of sushi, wonton, tempura (batter-fried vegetables), and kushi-sashi (skewered barbecued beef). Japanese beer, sake, and tea beverages complement each and every bite. Beginning at 4 P.M., teriyaki dinners are served, along with a variety of other sensational taste-tempting choices. A word of warning: dinner tickets must be purchased in advance.

Have you ever watched a bonsai being trimmed or experienced the beauty and simplicity of Asian flower arrangement? You'll encounter these and other special Japanese-oriented activities going on throughout the event. Additional programs include Asian and brush-painting exhibits, origami, block-printing demonstrations, and the sale of handmade gifts and crafts.

The festival ends in the evening with a performance of Obon Odori, traditional Japanese folk dancing. Everyone in attendance is encouraged to join in.

San Luis Obispo lies midway between San Francisco and Los Angeles on the California central coast. The city of San Luis Obispo lies along both sides of California Highway 101.

KUSHI-SASHI

Have butcher cut boneless beef into very thin slices. If slicing at home, partially freeze beef and cut thin. Thread beef onto bamboo skewers.

Bring all marinade ingredients to a boil, then simmer until thickened (about 1 hour). Dip beef into prepared teriyaki marinade. Grill over hot coals. The marinade is tasty used on chicken, pork, and fish.

Obon Festival
San Luis Obispo, CA

boneless beef (top sirloin), sliced very thin

Teriyaki Marinade

2 cups shoyu (soy sauce)

1 tablespoon freshly grated ginger

1 cup sugar

1 1/2 cups sake

1/4 teaspoon ajinomoto

GREEN BEANS WITH SESAME SEED SAUCE

1 pound green beans

2 tablespoons salt

Sesame Seed Sauce

3 tablespoons sesame seeds, toasted

1 tablespoon sugar

2 tablespoons mirin

2 tablespoons shoyu (soy sauce)

1/4 teaspoon ajinomoto

Remove strings and ends of beans. Cook beans in boiling salted water. Do not cover and do not overcook. Rinse with cold water and drain. Cut beans into 2-inch lengths.

Grind sesame seeds in suribachi (similar to a bowl and pestle) until fine. Add sugar, mirin, shoyu, and ajinomoto; mix well. Pour over green beans, mixing well.

Obon Festival
San Luis Obispo, CA

SOFT ASIAN BEEF TACOS

1 pound beef sirloin, cut into $^1/_8$-inch slices

$^2/_3$ cup teriyaki sauce

3 cloves garlic, minced

$^1/_2$ teaspoon crushed red pepper flakes

1 tablespoon cornstarch

2 tablespoons vegetable oil

8 ounces prepared broccoli coleslaw mixture (about 3 cups)

1 cup thinly sliced green onions

3 cups cooked rice

12 flour tortillas, warmed

Stack slices of beef and cut into thin $^1/_8$-inch matchstick strips. Transfer to large bowl. Add $^1/_3$ cup teriyaki sauce, garlic, and red pepper flakes; stir well. Cover and marinate in the refrigerator for 20 minutes. Combine cornstarch and remaining teriyaki sauce in small bowl; set aside. Heat large skillet or wok over medium-high heat until hot. Add 1 tablespoon oil to skillet, add beef in two batches. Cook each batch, stirring, 5 to 7 minutes until brown; remove from skillet, keep warm. Add remaining tablespoon of oil to skillet. Add coleslaw and green onions, stir-fry 3 to 5 minutes or until tender. Return beef to skillet, add teriyaki mixture, and bring to a boil for 1 minute. Stir in rice.

To warm tortillas, wrap in aluminum foil and heat for 15 minutes in a 325° oven. Place $^3/_4$ cup mixture in each warm tortilla, roll up, and serve.

U.S.A. Rice Council
Houston, TX

Substitute 3 cups chopped fresh or frozen vegetables for broccoli slaw mixture.

ASIAN SLAW

1/2 cup water

6 tablespoons sugar

6 tablespoons distilled white vinegar

1 package (about 1.4 ounces) dried shrimp

1/2 teaspoon salt

3 1/2 cups (10 ounces) finely shredded green cabbage

1 medium red onion, thinly sliced

1/3 cup sliced, pitted California ripe olives

In a 1- to 1 1/2-quart pan over medium heat, bring water and sugar to a boil, stirring until sugar dissolves. Remove pan from heat, add vinegar, shrimp, and salt. Let stand for 30 minutes to soften shrimp. In a large serving bowl, combine cabbage, onion, olives, and shrimp mixture. Mix gently. Serve at room temperature or cover and chill up to 4 hours to serve cold.

California Olive Industry
Fresno, CA

OLIVAS ADOBE FIESTA

VENTURA

Annual. First Saturday in July.

The historic Olivas Adobe serves as the setting for entertainment, food, tours, and demonstrations highlighting life during California's early rancho days. Pile the family in the car and enjoy a trip back into earlier times. You'll be able to taste authentic foods, and tour the famous adobe, and children of all ages will have a great time trying to break the piñata.

Traditional Latino and hearty rancho-style foods include such favorites as handmade tortillas, homemade tamales and nachos, plus Native American frybread. During the feasting, be sure to watch the volunteer docents as they prepare and demonstrate the cooking of bread in an horno. For the uninitiated, an horno is a dome-shaped oven, usually made of adobe and constructed in the outdoors or in an open area. It is used to bake bread by Mexican and Spanish cooks.

Throughout the fiesta, residents and docents also demonstrate quilt making, woodworking, spinning, pottery making, using leather tools, and corn grinding. Now and then, you may be asked to join in and try your hand during one of the educational and entertaining demonstrations.

(Continued)

During the day, trained docents conduct guided tours of the authentically restored, two-story adobe and its surrounding courtyard and garden. You'll see up-close the adobe's La Sala room, sewing room, dining room, kitchen, bedrooms, and family chapel. A small museum near the adobe exhibits several displays of early California rancho days.

Located along Highway 101, about 65 miles north of Los Angeles, Ventura dates back more than 200 years to when California mission founder Father Junipero Serra was looking for the ideal location to build another mission. Mission San Buenaventura is the ninth and last mission founded by him. Olivas Adobe Historical Park is located at 4200 Olivas Park Drive.

All of the recipes in the Olivas Adobe section are from the *Mexican Cookery* cookbook. The Adobe's volunteer docents gathered together favorite ranch-style recipes that make up their fund-raising cookbook.

FLAN

Caramel Pudding

Heat 1/2 cup of sugar in a small skillet until a light brown syrup forms. Spread evenly on sides and bottom of custard pan while still hot. Cool. Beat eggs, add 1 cup sugar gradually, then milk, salt, and vanilla. Pour mixture into pan containing burnt sugar and set in a pan of water. Bake in moderate 350° oven for about 30 minutes, or until a knife inserted in center comes out clean. Chill in the refrigerator. To serve, unmold by running a knife between the custard and the pan. Then place a serving dish upside down over the pan and invert quickly.

1 1/2 cups sugar

5 eggs

1 1/2 quarts milk

1/4 teaspoon salt

1 teaspoon vanilla

SOFT CRAB TACOS WITH CITRUS SALSA

2 tablespoons olive oil

1 clove garlic, minced or pressed

1 small red onion, finely chopped

1 large firm ripe tomato, cored, chopped

1 4-ounce can diced green chilies

1 pound crab, shelled, cooked

12 corn tortillas (6 inch size)

salt to taste

Salsa

½ cup chopped cucumber

1 fresh jalapeño chili, stemmed, seeded, minced

1 cup diced canned or fresh pineapple

1 tablespoon lime peel, grated

3 tablespoons lime juice

2 tablespoons minced fresh cilantro

In a 10-inch or 12-inch pan over medium-high heat, combine oil, garlic, and onion. Cook until onion begins to brown, 8 to 10 minutes. Add tomato and chilies, simmer until tomato is soft, 8 to 10 minutes. Remove from heat, add crab. Meanwhile, stack tortillas, wrap in foil, and warm in a 350° oven for about 10 minutes.

Mix all salsa ingredients together.

Spoon crab filling onto tortilla, add salsa and salt to taste. Fold in half to enclose filling. Repeat for remaining tacos.

CHICKEN SALAD BURRITO

In medium bowl, combine sour cream, taco sauce, cumin, and chili powder. Add chicken, avocado, tomato, and chilies. Gently toss to mix. Place 1/4 cup of salad mixture and some lettuce on each flour tortilla, fold bottom up and over salad mixture. Fold sides in and roll up until salad mixture is enclosed completely.

Wrap each burrito in clear plastic wrap to hold its shape until ready to serve.

6 tablespoons sour cream

1/4 cup hot taco sauce

1 teaspoon cumin

3/4 teaspoon chili powder

1 5-ounce can chunk white chicken, diced

1/2 cup chopped avocado

1/2 cup chopped tomatoes

2 tablespoons diced Ortega chiles

6 flour tortillas

1/4 cup shredded lettuce

TORTILLA HASH

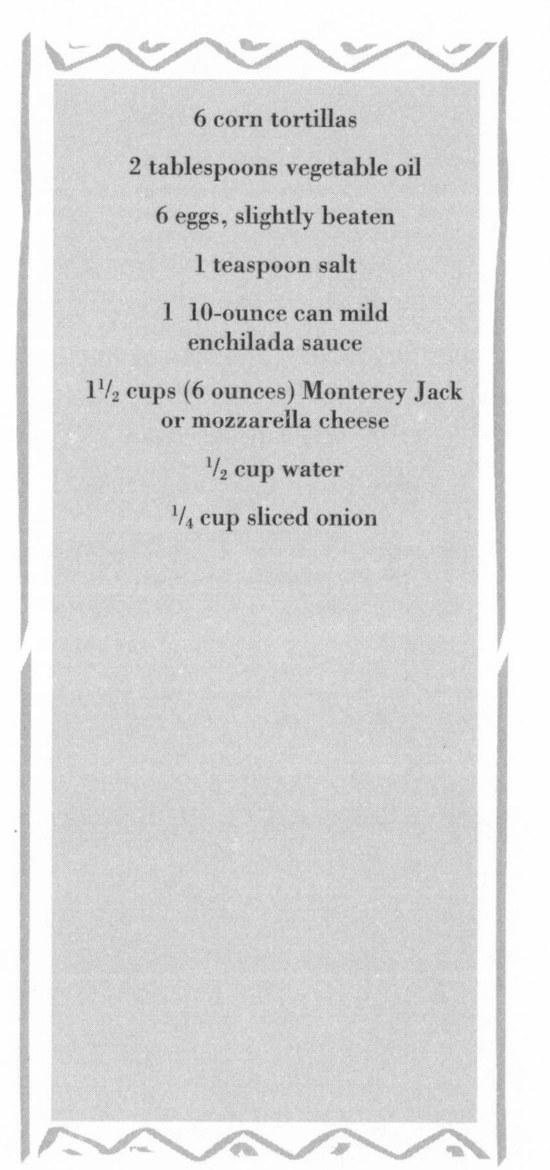

6 corn tortillas

2 tablespoons vegetable oil

6 eggs, slightly beaten

1 teaspoon salt

1 10-ounce can mild enchilada sauce

$1\frac{1}{2}$ cups (6 ounces) Monterey Jack or mozzarella cheese

$\frac{1}{2}$ cup water

$\frac{1}{4}$ cup sliced onion

Tear tortillas into $1\frac{1}{2}$-inch pieces. Fry tortilla pieces in 1 inch hot oil until crisp and golden. Remove with slotted spoon. Reserve 2 tablespoons oil in skillet and return tortillas to skillet. Stir in eggs and salt. Cook and stir until tortilla pieces are coated and eggs are set. Stir in enchilada sauce, 1 cup cheese, water, and half the onion. Simmer uncovered for 15 minutes. Spoon into serving dish. Top with remaining cheese and onion.

ORANGE BLOSSOM FESTIVAL

RIVERSIDE

Annual. Spring date varies.

Interested in a festival with a tangy twist? The Orange Blossom Festival celebrates more than one hundred years of Riverside's citrus heritage. It's a two-day, family event held along twenty blocks of the city's historic downtown streets.

If you want to discover a plethora of fascinating orange-inspired cuisine, head for Gourmet Grove. Dozens of participating southern California chefs create their specialities and sell them to festival-goers. Afterward, head for the celebrity chef demonstrations, where you'll marvel at food preparation tips and techniques, observe noted carvers shape ice into intricate sculptures, and have a chance to talk to and observe celebrity chefs in action. In addition, the Food Emporium includes several concessionaires, each serving at least one orange-based food item.

During the festival, you'll discover a wide variety of entertainment diversions. Talented, costumed performers stroll the streets, bicycles and antique cars replace modern-day automobiles, and the air is perfumed with the scent of orange blossoms.

Children's Grove features slices of art and fun for the kids. They can pick from craft projects; elephant, camel, or llama rides; or friendly animals at the petting zoo. The whole family will enjoy day-long performances by puppeteers, magicians, mimes, jugglers, and clowns. Face painters create orangelike cheeks, while balloon artists twist their air-filled sculptures into intriguing shapes.

(Continued)

If you're a history buff, step back into history by visiting recreated turn-of-the-century programs, including gold panning, basketweaving demonstrations, and Indian baking and corn roasting. You'll find yourself reliving part of Riverside's rich, citrus-flavored history.

The event and entertainment schedule for Sunkist's Orange Blossom Festival is varied and long. You'll be glad you decided to attend this flavorful celebration of Southern California's citrus heritage.

CUMIN CHICKEN WITH HOT CITRUS SALSA

Combine the tomato halves and boiling water and allow to rest 10 minutes; drain and chop. Combine with orange, cilantro, jalapeños, and ginger, and set aside. Combine cumin, salt, and pepper and rub into chicken. Cook chicken in hot oil, 3 minutes on each side. Serve over hot rice. Spoon prepared salsa over chicken breast.

Pat Paulsen, First Prize Winner
Sunkist Orange Blossom Festival
Riverside, CA

4 dried tomato halves

1/4 cup boiling water

1 medium orange, peeled, chopped, reserve 2 teaspoons juice

2 teaspoons snipped cilantro

1/2 teaspoon minced, seeded jalapeños

1 teaspoon grated ginger root

3/4 teaspoon cumin

1/8 teaspoon salt

1/8 teaspoon pepper

2 chicken breast halves, skinned, boned

1 tablespoon cooking oil

VEAL CHOPS WITH ORANGE THYME JUS

2 12-ounce veal chops

2 ounces orange juice

6 ounces wild mushrooms

1 ounce olive oil

shallots

garlic

salt

pepper

dash lemon juice

1 segmented orange, reserve juice for sauce

1 tablespoon fresh thyme

4 ounces favorite meat sauce

Marinate chops in orange juice. In skillet, sear chops until golden brown on both sides. Separately sauté mushrooms in olive oil with shallots, garlic, salt and pepper, and a touch of lemon juice. Add sautéed mushroom mixture, reserved orange juice, and thyme to chops. Cook 7 to 10 minutes. Add meat sauce, reduce to desired consistency, and season to taste. Serve by placing veal chops, orange segments, and mushrooms on plate. Strain sauce and spoon over veal chops.

Executive Chef Joe E. Cochran, Jr.
Mission Inn
Riverside, CA

ORANGE GROVE PIE

For the meringue: Beat egg whites until foamy, add cream of tartar and beat to stiff peaks. Gradually add one cup of sugar, continue beating to very stiff peaks.

Heat oven to 275°. Grease a 9-inch pie plate just to edge, sprinkle edge with finely chopped walnuts. Fill with meringue. Bake for 1 hour.

For the filling: Beat egg yolks slightly and add sugar, lemon juice, and grated orange rind. Cook over boiling water, stirring constantly until thickened, about 10 minutes. Fold in 2 of the oranges that have been peeled and diced. Cool and fold in 1 cup of the whipped cream. Pour into center of meringue pie, smooth top, chill at least 12 hours or longer.

Before serving, top with mounds of whipped cream, leaving room for center to be filled with remaining 3 oranges that have been peeled and sectioned. Top with grated orange rind.

Claudia Amici, 1st Place Winner
Sunkist Orange Blossom Festival
Riverside, CA

Meringue

4 egg whites

1¼ teaspoons cream of tartar

1 cup sugar

5 tablespoons finely crushed walnuts

Filling

5 egg yolks

½ cup sugar

2 tablespoons lemon juice

3 tablespoons grated orange peel

5 oranges, peeled and diced

1 pint heavy cream, whipped

PIE FESTIVAL

MALIBU

Annual. First Saturday in October.

Malibu is well known as a famous retreat for movie stars, sun worshipers, and surfers. It is little known, though, that some of California's best-tasting pies are found at the Malibu Pie Festival. Each year, children bob for apples, youngsters and Pepperdine University students strive for the fastest pie consumption at the pie eating contest, and everyone enjoys a slice of home-baked pie. Festival organizers refer to this day-long event as the Festival of Fun and Good Taste.

During the frantic pie eating contests no utensils are allowed, so it takes imagination and creativity to be a winner. The participants go for speed, and viewers have one peach-of-a-time watching the antics.

You'll want to save room to taste more than one piece of the tantalizingly tempting baked pies. Dozens of local residents enter their favorite pie in a competition. Judging is done by celebrities, business and civic leaders, and guest judges.

When you're ready to take a break from consuming some of the best pies around, you can enjoy a celebrity pie auction, a silent auction, have your face painted, buy a pie to take home, and shop for pie festival T-shirts, aprons, and pie plates.

This hometown-style, tasty celebration benefits Malibu children and family programs, including a nursery school, a campout for dads and kids, and the Tales-by-the-Sea storytelling concert series.

The location of this festival may change, so contact the organizers (see Information Directory) for the current information.

PEANUT BUTTER CREAM PIE

Blend first 3 ingredients with fork until crumbly. Reserve 3 tablespoons for decorating top. Bake pie shell until lightly browned.

Stir together sugar, cornstarch, and salt in saucepan. Blend milk and egg yolks, gradually stir into sugar mixture. Cook over medium heat, stirring constantly, until mixture thickens and boils. Boil and stir 1 minute. Remove from heat, blend in butter and vanilla. Immediately pour into baked pie shell, press plastic wrap over filling. Chill pie thoroughly, at least 2 hours.

Whip 1 cup of whipping cream and pile on top of cooled filling. Decorate with reserved sugar mixture.

Diane Jenson, First Place Winner
Malibu Pie Festival
Malibu, CA

Sugar Mixture

1 9-inch baked pie shell, broken into pieces (see Mrs. Bixler's Famous Pie Crust, next recipe)

3/4 cup confectioners sugar

1/3 cup peanut butter

Cream Filling

2/3 cup sugar

1/4 cup cornstarch

1/2 teaspoon salt

3 cups milk

4 egg yolks, slightly beaten

2 tablespoons butter or margarine, softened

4 teaspoons vanilla

1 cup whipping cream for topping

MRS. BIXLER'S FAMOUS PIE CRUST

4 cups flour

1$^{3}/_{4}$ cups Crisco shortening

1 tablespoon sugar

1$^{1}/_{2}$ teaspoons salt

1 tablespoon vinegar

1 egg

$^{1}/_{2}$ cup water

Mix flour, Crisco, sugar, and salt in a bowl with a fork. In a separate bowl, beat vinegar, egg, and water. Add to flour mixture. Stir with fork until all ingredients are moist. Shape dough into a ball and chill for 15 minutes before rolling. This recipe makes 4 crusts.

Diane Jenson, First Place Winner
(Mrs. Bixler's daughter)
Malibu, CA

CHOCOLATE-RASPBERRY CREAM PIE

Crumble wafers and stir in melted butter; press into pie tin and bake at 350° for 20 minutes.

Spoon chocolate pudding into cooled shell, spreading over bottom and up sides. Gently spread vanilla pudding over chocolate pudding. Whip cream and pipe onto pie with pastry bag (star tip). Leave a 3-inch area in center. Place raspberries in center, sprinkle shaved chocolate over whipped cream. Keep chilled.

Wendy Knight, winner
Malibu Pie Festival
Malibu, CA

Crust

1 package chocolate wafers

1/2 stick butter, melted

Filling

1 cup chocolate pudding

1 cup vanilla pudding

1/2 pint heavy whipping cream

1/4 pint liqueur (optional) for soaking berries

1/2 cup fresh raspberries, rinsed, drained

shaved chocolate for topping decoration

FRESH LEMON MERINGUE PIE

1 1/2 cups sugar

1/4 cup plus 2 tablespoons cornstarch

1/4 teaspoon salt

1/2 cup cold water

1/2 cup fresh squeezed lemon juice

3 egg yolks, well beaten

2 tablespoons butter or margarine

1 1/2 cups boiling water

grated peel of 1/2 lemon

2 or 3 drops yellow food coloring (optional)

1 9-inch baked pie crust

Three-Egg Meringue

3 egg whites

1/4 teaspoon cream of tartar

6 tablespoon sugar

In 2- or 3-quart saucepan, thoroughly combine sugar, cornstarch, and salt. Gradually blend in cold water and lemon juice with wire whisk. Stir in egg yolks. Add butter and boiling water. Bring to boil over medium-high heat, stirring constantly with rubber spatula. Reduce heat to medium and boil for 1 minute. Remove from heat, stir in lemon peel and food coloring. Pour in baked pie crust. Let stand, allowing a thin film to form, while preparing meringue. Top with three-egg meringue, sealing well at edges. Bake at 350° for 12 to 15 minutes. Cool for 2 1/2 to 3 hours before serving.

Three-Egg Meringue: In bowl, with electric mixer, beat 3 egg whites with 1/4 teaspoon cream of tarter until foamy. Gradually add 6 tablespoons sugar and beat until stiff peaks form.

Sunkist Growers, Inc.
Van Nuys, CA

SUMMER SUNSHINE FRUIT

To prepare crust, mix flour, sugar, and grated lemon peel in a food processor or bowl. Add butter, whirl or rub with your fingers until fine crumbs form. Add egg, whirl or stir with a fork until dough holds together. Pat into a smooth ball.

Press dough over bottom and up sides of a greased and floured 10½- to 11-inch tart pan with removable rim. Bake in a 300° oven until pale gold (about 35 minutes); let cool.

To prepare filling, mix sugar and cornstarch, divide into 3 equal portions. In blender or food processor, purée nectarines with 1 tablespoon lemon juice and 1 portion of the sugar mixture until smooth; pour into a 1- to 3-quart pan.

Rinse blender, purée raspberries with 1 tablespoon lemon juice and 1 portion of the sugar mixture until smooth. Press through a fine strainer into another 1- to 3-quart pan. Discard seeds.

Rinse blender and strainer. Purée blackberries with remaining lemon juice and sugar mixture until smooth. Press through a fine strainer into another 1- to 3-quart pan. Discard seeds.

Stir mixtures one at a time over medium-high heat—start with nectarines, which darken—until bubbling vigorously, 3 to 5 minutes. As cooked, place pans in larger bowls of ice water. Stir often until mixtures are thick enough to flow heavily when pans are tilted, 5 to 10 minutes.

Spoon mixtures into alternating, parallel bands crust in, making 2 or 3 bands of each flavor. Pile more of the same flavor onto each band if you have extra. Pull tip of a chopstick or knife across bands, drawing one color into the next. Wipe tip of tool between pulls. You can alternate direction of pulls, or make all in one direction. Chill pie, uncovered, until set to touch, at least 3 hours. If made ahead, cover and chill until the next day. To serve, remove from pan and set on a platter.

Trinity Peacock-Broyles, First Place Winner
Pie Festival, children's category

Press-in Lemon Crust

1½ cups all-purpose flour

¼ cup sugar

1½ teaspoons grated lemon peel

1 cup butter or margarine, cut into small pieces

1 large egg

Filling

9 tablespoons sugar

⅓ cup cornstarch

2 cups peeled, pitted, chopped nectarines

3 tablespoons lemon juice, divided

2½ cups raspberries, rinsed and drained

2½ cups blackberries or boysenberries, rinsed and drained

PITCHIN', COOKIN', & SPITTIN' HULLABALOO

CALICO

Annual. Friday-Sunday, Palm Sunday weekend.

Calico's Pitchin', Cookin', & Spittin' Hullabaloo is three days of stew cooking, flapjack racing, and horseshoe pitching. One of many highlights during the event is the World Tobacco Spitting Championships. You have to agree, it's not every festival that can lay claim to that!

Anyone who thinks they have a winning stew is welcome to enter the Old Miner's Stew Cook-off and compete for awards and recognition. There's plenty of stiff competition by amateur cooks from all over the southland, but the excitement makes it all worthwhile. Entries vary each year, but expect to find plenty of taste-tempting variety.

Does your wardrobe include boots, jeans, bandanas, and a Stetson? If so, wear them and you'll fit right in and have a rip-roaring good time. Heck, try some boot scootin' and lasso tossin' while getting a view and taste of the Old West.

While the stew's cooking, you'll hear some mighty fine bluegrass and country music being played in locations scattered around Main Street. But, watch out for the gunfights and high-stepping saloon dancers.

This rip-roaring festival is your invitation to venture back to the old days and relive the pioneer spirit. It's your chance to have a high-stepping good time, learn about old-time silver mining, partake of hearty food, and do it all in a real ghost town.

CALICO BAKED BEANS

Cook hamburger, onion, and bacon. Set aside. Mix all remaining ingredients, add to meat, and bake in an ovenproof casserole at 350° for one hour.

Cindy Looney, contributor
Recipes from Across the United States
Kewanee, IL

1/2 to 1 pound hamburger
1 onion, diced
1/2 pound bacon, chopped
1/4 cup brown sugar
1/4 cup sugar
1/4 cup catsup
1/4 cup barbecue sauce
1 teaspoon pepper
1 teaspoon salt
1/2 teaspoon chili powder or to taste
1 can kidney beans
1 can butter beans
1 can pork and beans

BEEF WINE STEW

1¼ pounds lean beef, cut into 1-inch cubes

vegetable oil spray

1½ cups chopped onion

1 cup chopped green onion

2 or 3 potatoes, peeled and cut into 1-inch pieces

1 cup sliced celery

1 pound carrots, peeled, cut into 1-inch pieces

4 cups water

2 cups dry red wine

salt and pepper to taste

2 tablespoons cornstarch

¼ cup cold water

Sauté beef in 5-quart pan coated with vegetable oil spray. Add onions and green pepper. Cook, stirring often, until vegetables are tender. Add potatoes, celery, carrots, water, wine, salt, and pepper, and bring to a boil. Reduce heat, cover, and simmer 1½ hours. Blend cornstarch with ¼ cup cold water and gradually stir into boiling stew. Cook over medium-high heat, stirring constantly until thickened and bubbly.

Cindy Looney, contributor
Recipes from Across the United States
Kewanee, IL

DAD'S FAVORITE CROCKPOT STEW

In crockpot, alternate beef and onions (stick cloves into one of the onions). Sprinkle with sugar and salt. Mix gravy sauce, vinegar, bay leaf, thyme, garlic, and water together. Pour over meat and onions. Cover, cook on low for 5 to 7 hours, or until tender. Turn control to high. Dissolve flour in small amount of water and add to meat juices. Stir occasionally while cooking on high for final 15 to 20 minutes. Remove cloves before serving.

Bob Carter
Oxnard, CA

2 pounds beef stew meat, cut into 1½-inch cubes

12 to 14 small white onions

4 whole cloves

2 tablespoons brown sugar

1½ teaspoons salt

½ teaspoon gravy sauce

1 tablespoon red wine vinegar

1 bay leaf

⅛ teaspoon thyme

garlic, minced, to taste

¾ cup water

¼ cup flour

OXTAIL STEW

4 pounds oxtails, cut into 2-inch pieces

1/4 cup flour

salt and pepper to taste

2 tablespoons salad oil

1 medium tomato, peeled, chopped

1 onion, chopped

3 carrots, chopped

2 turnips, chopped

1 clove garlic, crushed

1 bay leaf

3 cups beef bouillon

1 cup port wine

2 leeks, sliced, white portions only

Coat meat with flour, salt, and pepper. Sauté meat in oil until brown. Remove meat to crock pot with a slotted spoon, add all other ingredients, cover, and cook on low for 7 to 9 hours. Discard bay leaf, remove oxtails, cut and scrape meat off the bones. Dice the meat and return to stew. Cool slightly and skim off any excess fat before serving.

Some unknown cowboy must have developed this easy and tasty stew. I found this handwritten recipe tucked away in an old thrift shop cookbook.

RAISIN FESTIVAL

SELMA

Annual. First Saturday in May.

The folks around Selma pull out all the stops and make a special effort to entertain and feed you during their raisin harvest season. More than 95 percent of the raisins grown in the United States come from within a 40-mile radius of Selma. It's only fitting the small community bill itself as the Raisin Capital of the World.

You'll love this homegrown event. Local non-profit groups serve some of the best food around. Baking contests for junior and adult competitors include cookies with raisins, cookies without raisins, cakes, yeast breads, quick breads, pies with raisins and pies without raisins. Here's the best part: you can purchase samples of the entries and see how your taste stacks up with that of the judges.

Even if you aren't a connoisseur of great art, you know what you like, and that makes you eligible to help select the People's Choice award during the art competition. The public also helps select the artwork that best represents the festival's Raisin Country theme. Wouldn't you know it, there's even a special category of art that must include raisins as part of its execution.

If you're a green thumb, don't miss viewing the entries in the floriculture contest. Local residents create and exhibit some spectacular arrangements using fresh-cut flowers, green plants, and flowering plants. Perhaps it's the area's combination of spring rains and summer sunshine that help produce some of the prize specimens.

(Continued)

Raisin Royalty takes center stage as residents compete to wear the queen's crown. A professionally produced carnival provides midway fun with thrill rides, carnival games, and kiddie attractions.

When you feel like taking a day to enjoy some simple family fun, pack up the car, head to Selma, and take in a day celebrating the wrinkled grape. Join in or watch as local entertainment—bands, dancers, mariachis, and magicians—perform their feats and display their talents.

While you're in the area, be sure to drive the few short miles from Selma and visit the Sun Maid Growers Store. There you'll discover everything to satisfy any raisin lover's fantasies. Selma is located about 16 miles south of Fresno, off U.S. Highway 101.

RAISIN DATE BARS

Filling

3 cups cut-up dates

1/4 cup sugar

1 1/2 cups water

1 cup raisins

Crumble Mixture

1/2 cup margarine, softened

1/4 cup shortening

1 cup packed brown sugar

1 3/4 cups flour

1 teaspoon salt

1/2 teaspoon baking soda

1 1/2 cups quick-cooking oats

Filling: Mix dates, sugar, and water in saucepan. Cook over low heat, stirring occasionally, about 10 minutes, until thickened. Cool. Add raisins and stir.

Crumble Mixture: Cream margarine, shortening, and sugar. Mix in remaining ingredients.

Press half the crumble mixture evenly in bottom of 13x9-inch greased pan. Spread with filling. Top with remaining crumble mixture, pressing lightly. Bake 15 to 20 minutes at 400°, until light brown. While warm, cut into bars. Makes 3 dozen cookies.

Stacy Ekberg, First Place Winner
Selma Raisin Festival, Junior Division Cookie Contest

QUICK SOUR CREAM RAISIN BREAD

1½ cups flour

1 cup loosely packed brown sugar

½ teaspoon baking soda

2 teaspoons baking powder

¼ teaspoon salt

1 cup sour cream

2 eggs

Streusel

2 tablespoons flour

4 tablespoons brown sugar

1 teaspoon cinnamon

2 tablespoons margarine

1 cup raisins

Mix flour, brown sugar, baking soda, baking powder, and salt. Whip together sour cream and eggs. Mix with dry ingredients. Spread in lightly greased 9x9-inch pan. Blend streusel ingredients until crumbly. Sprinkle over bread. Bake at 350° for 15 to 20 minutes.

Stacy Ekberg, First Place Winner
Selma Raisin Festival, Junior Division Baking Contest

RAPID RAISIN SAUCE

- $^1/_2$ cup brown sugar
- $^1/_2$ tablespoon mustard
- $^1/_2$ tablespoon flour
- $^1/_4$ cup seedless raisins
- $^1/_4$ cup vinegar
- $1^3/_4$ cups water

Mix brown sugar, mustard, and flour; add raisins, vinegar, and water. Cook slowly in a saucepan until mixture becomes the consistency of syrup.

Terry Poland
Oxnard, CA

Try this sauce poured over ham or tongue.

MORNING GLORY MUFFINS

½ cup raisins

2 cups all-purpose flour

1 cup sugar

2 teaspoons baking soda

2 teaspoons cinnamon

½ teaspoon salt

2 cups grated peeled carrots

1 large tart green apple, cored and grated

½ cup chopped walnuts

½ cup sweetened shredded coconut

3 eggs

⅔ cup vegetable oil

2 teaspoon vanilla

Soak raisins in hot water for 30 minutes and drain. Line muffin pan with paper baking cups. Mix flour, sugar, baking soda, cinnamon, and salt in a bowl. Stir in raisins, carrots, apple, walnuts, and coconut. Beat eggs with oil and vanilla to blend. Stir into flour mixture until just combined. Divide batter into muffin cups. Bake until golden brown (20 to 22 minutes). Cool 5 minutes. Remove from pan, and enjoy.

Susan Melgoza, First Place Winner
Selma Raisin Festival, Baking Contest

REDEDICATION CELEBRATION

ALLENSWORTH

Annual. October weekend varies.

It seems to me that it's a great idea to stop, reflect, and honor something at least once a year. That's what folks do annually during this fitting celebration honoring Allensworth State Historic Park.

In the early 1900s, Colonel Allensworth established a town for African-Americans that would be self-governing. The town was the realization of his dream. The area is now preserved as Colonel Allensworth State Historic Park.

You won't want to miss out on any of the fun activities of the day. During this special day, there are docent-led tours where you'll learn much about African-American culture, the original town's people, and their commitment and optimism. You'll hear exciting, time-honored anecdotes that bring to life the park's two-room schoolhouse, general store, post office, hotel, town library, and the original founder's home.

You'll get a chance to enjoy some mighty fine jazz, blues, and gospel music, ethnic and eclectic food, and art and crafts. Vendors display and sell their wares, and dozens of participants provide plenty of imaginative culinary delights. Both young and old can participate in historical games and take in special exhibits on African-American history. Everyone is invited to wear authentic 1908 to 1918 attire, in keeping with the spirit of the day.

(Continued)

There is only one place like it in all of California, so this historic park is well worth a visit. Allensworth is approximately 75 miles south of Fresno and 38 miles north of Bakersfield. Too few people know about it, but word is finally getting around.

Sally Clipps works for the California Department of Parks and Recreation. An active supporter of Allensworth State Historic Park, she provided the recipes for this section.

DIRTY RICE

Place chicken gizzards in a small saucepan. Add water to cover, bring to a boil, and simmer 30 minutes. In a Dutch oven, heat the oil, add the chicken livers, sauté until cooked. Remove from pan and reserve. Add ground beef, onion, bell pepper, celery, garlic, salt, and pepper to the pot. Sauté until the meat is no longer pink and vegetables are tender. Chop the cooked gizzards and chicken livers very fine. Add them to the pot along with the water and rice. Stir to mix. Bring to a boil, lower heat, and simmer 30 minutes or until rice is cooked. Add chopped green onions and parsley. Let stand 10 minutes, covered, before serving. Garnish with additional bell pepper.

3 chicken gizzards

water

2 tablespoons oil

2 chicken livers

1/2 pound ground beef

1 onion, chopped

1 bell pepper, chopped
(save a little for garnish)

1 stalk celery, chopped

2 cloves garlic, chopped

pinch salt and cayenne pepper
to taste

2 cups water

1 cup uncooked long grain rice

3 green onions, chopped

1 tablespoon parsley

BLACKEYE PEAS

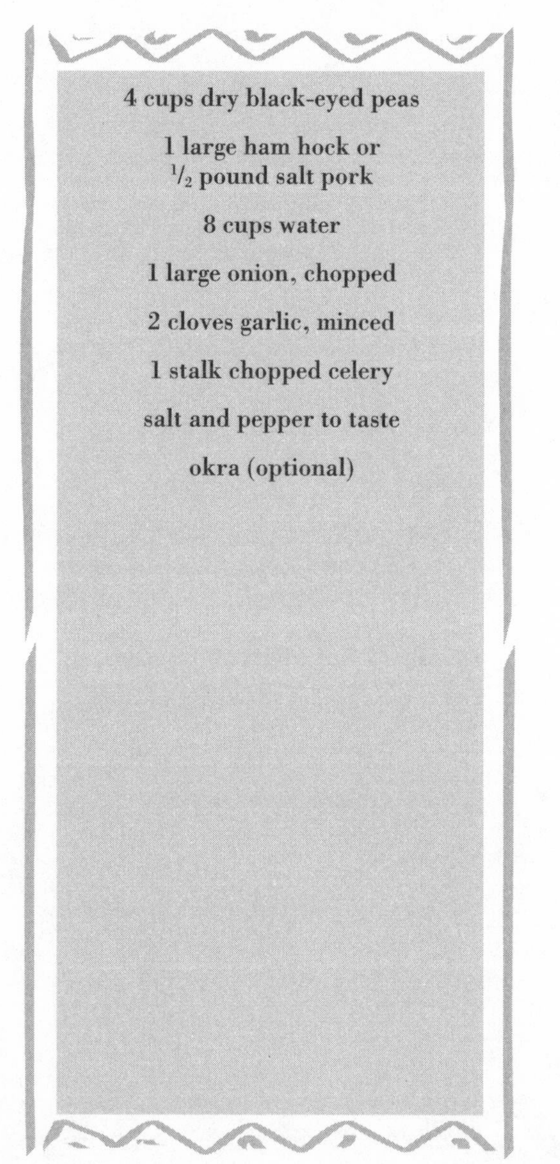

4 cups dry black-eyed peas

1 large ham hock or
1/2 pound salt pork

8 cups water

1 large onion, chopped

2 cloves garlic, minced

1 stalk chopped celery

salt and pepper to taste

okra (optional)

Soak black-eyed peas overnight. Cook ham hock or salt pork until tender. Add peas, onion, garlic, celery, salt, and pepper. Cook until peas are tender. Serve over rice. For variation, add okra on top of peas the last 10 minutes.

TEA CAKES

Heat oven to 350°. Grease cookie sheet. Beat sugar and margarine in large bowl with electric mixer on medium speed until light and fluffy. Add eggs, 1 at a time, beating well after each addition. Gradually add flour, salt, and baking soda, beating until smooth. Stir in vanilla and lemon extract. Roll dough on lightly floured surface until about 1/2-inch thick, adding flour to prevent sticking. Cut with floured cookie or biscuit cutter and place on cookie sheet. Bake 8 to 10 minutes. Remove from cookie sheet to cool on wire rack. Sprinkle with sugar before serving.

1 2/3 cups sugar

2 sticks margarine or butter, softened

2 eggs

3 1/2 cups flour

dash salt

1/2 teaspoon baking soda

1 1/2 teaspoons vanilla

1/2 teaspoon lemon extract or lemon juice

MIXED GREENS

1/2 pound Canadian bacon, sliced

2 tablespoons oil

2 cloves garlic, minced

1 medium onion, chopped

2 cups water

3 large bunches collard greens, chopped

1/2 head cabbage, chopped

Add bacon, oil, garlic, and onion to water in medium-large saucepan. Cook 20 minutes. Add collard greens and cook until tender, about 20 minutes. Add chopped cabbage and cook with lid on for 10 minutes. Serve with hush puppies (recipe follows) or corn bread.

HUSH PUPPIES

Combine cornmeal, baking powder, salt, and onions. Beat the egg and milk together, add to the dry ingredients, and mix. Shape into 1/2-inch-thick patties. Deep-fry at 370° until golden brown. Drain on paper towel and serve hot.

1 cup cornmeal

1/2 teaspoon double-acting baking powder

1/2 teaspoon salt

2 tablespoons minced onions

1 egg

1/4 cup milk

RENAISSANCE PLEASURE FAIRE

SAN BERNARDINO COUNTY

Annual. 9 weekends, April-June.

34

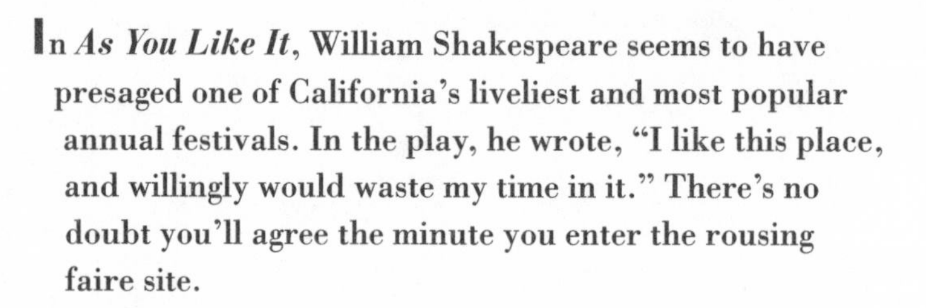

In *As You Like It*, William Shakespeare seems to have presaged one of California's liveliest and most popular annual festivals. In the play, he wrote, "I like this place, and willingly would waste my time in it." There's no doubt you'll agree the minute you enter the rousing faire site.

The Renaissance Pleasure Faire creates a 16th-century English country fair and marketplace. During each day, more than 1,200 costumed actors, minstrels, dancers, and musicians join hundreds of cooks, crafters, and beverage purveyors to entertain and delight faire visitors.

Each year, one weekend is designated for an amateur cooking and homebrewing competition. Entries are accepted in four categories: Meat Dishes and Stews; Sweets, Pasterries, and Savouries; Vegetables and Sallets; and Illusion Foods. Rules require that all entrants transport and serve their entries without refrigeration or reheating. After all, this is the 16th-century!

Feasting at the faire includes a variety of traditional English fare, and each year's menu offers traditional shepherd's pies, Cornish pasties, bangers with grilled onions, batter-fried English fish'n' chips, hearty ales, fresh juices, and fine wines. In addition, you'll discover a selection of foods from distant lands, including New

World roasted turkey legs and corn on the cob drenched in sweet butter, berries in frozen cream, and French crêpes filled with sweet creams and fruits.

In addition to plenty of feasting, time-travelers at the faire can enjoy jousting tournaments, spectacular processions, Shakespearean scenes, and enough entertainment to last an Elizabethan lifetime. Players present lively historical reenactments of the lifestyles of Elizabethan citizenry, from peasant and servant to noble, soldier, merchant, and fool.

Bring the kids. A special delight for young knights and gentle maidens are the authentic Elizabethan games and handmade toys, plus participation in a fairy tale theatre, arts, crafts, and the magic of puppetry.

In southern California, the Renaissance Pleasure Faire takes place at Glen Helen Regional Park located at 2555 Devore Road in Devore, near the intersection of California Highways 15 and 215.

GOLDEN APPLES OF MEAT

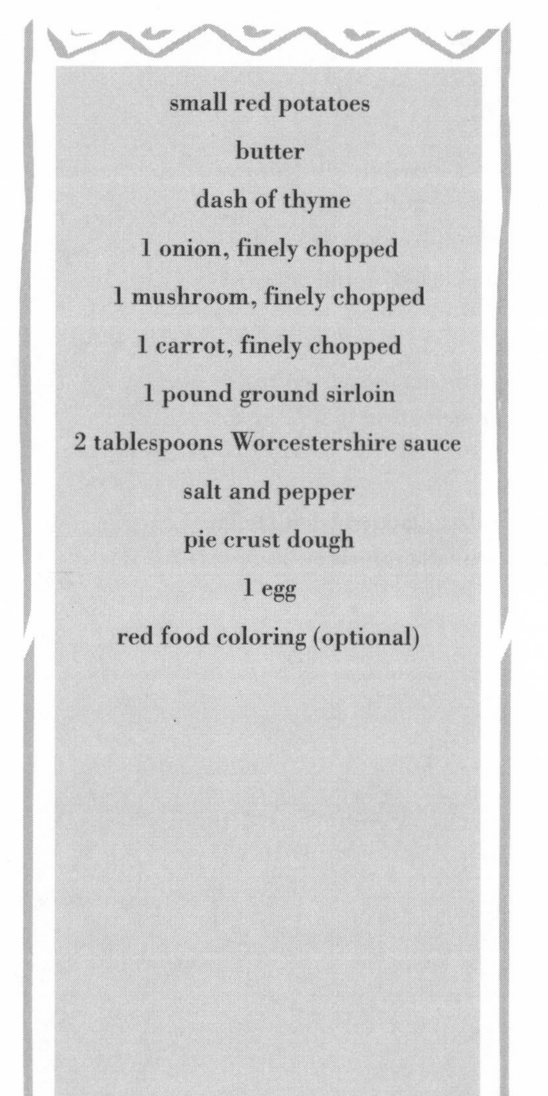

small red potatoes
butter
dash of thyme
1 onion, finely chopped
1 mushroom, finely chopped
1 carrot, finely chopped
1 pound ground sirloin
2 tablespoons Worcestershire sauce
salt and pepper
pie crust dough
1 egg
red food coloring (optional)

Bake potatoes in ovenproof dish with butter and thyme for about 15 minutes or until tender. Set aside and allow to cool. Sauté onion, mushroom, and carrot in butter for 1 minute. Add to ground sirloin. Add Worcestershire sauce, and salt and pepper to taste. Wrap meat mixture around the potatoes to form meatballs with potatoes in center. Fry meatballs in skillet until brown. Wrap meatballs in pie crust dough and mold into apple shapes. Brush with beaten egg and bake at 375° for about 20 minutes. When removed from oven, brush with a small amount of red food coloring, if desired.

Louise Jurgens
Renaissance Pleasure Faire

EGGS IN FRENCH ROLLS

4 French rolls

butter for spreading

8 eggs

juice from 1 or 2 oranges

Cut the rolls in half lengthwise and scoop out some of the center bread. Toast the insides and spread with butter. Break an egg into each half roll and season with salt and pepper. Bake at 350° approximately 20 to 30 minutes or until the eggs are set. Sprinkle the orange juice over the eggs and serve very hot.

Renaissance Pleasure Faire
San Bernardino, CA

Legend has it that Hannah Glasse prepared this hot feasting for her family in the early 1700s.

SCULPTURED HONEY WHOLE WHEAT BREAD

$^1/_2$ cup warm water

2 envelopes yeast

$^1/_2$ cup honey

$1^1/_2$ cups milk

4 ounces clotted cream or cream cheese

3 cups whole-wheat flour

$^1/_2$ cup wheat germ

$1^1/_2$ teaspoons salt

2 to $2^1/_2$ cups all-purpose flour

1 tablespoon water

Sprinkle yeast over warm water in a 2-cup measuring cup. Stir in 1 teaspoon of the honey. Stir to dissolve and let stand 10 minutes.

In medium-size saucepan heat milk and cream cheese until well blended, cool to lukewarm. Stir in yeast mixture. Stir in whole wheat flour, wheat germ, and salt until smooth. Stir in enough flour to make a soft dough. Knead until smooth and elastic (10 minutes). Place in large buttered bowl, cover with a damp towel, and let rise about 1 hour or until doubled in bulk. Punch down and turn onto floured surface. Knead a few times, cover with bowl to rest 10 minutes. Butter pan, shape dough to desired sculpture. Cover with towel and let rise in warm place 45 minutes. Combine water and remaining honey, brush on bread. Bake in pre-heated oven at 325° for 45 minutes.

Lisa Lennaco
Renaissance Pleasure Faire

SCANDINAVIAN FESTIVAL

THOUSAND OAKS

Annual. Third Saturday in April.

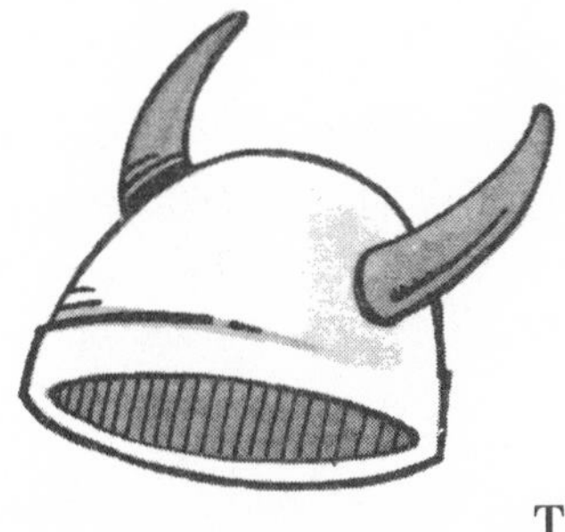

The Scandinavian Festival honors rich Scandinavian traditions as well as the founders of California Lutheran University. One of the oldest festivals in California, this is also the largest Scandinavian/Baltic celebration in the state. It's a family-style banquet for your eyes, ears, and taste buds. There's plenty to enjoy including creative food demonstrations, theatrical and musical performances, celebrated lecturers, and impressive arts and crafts. You can either sit back and watch the sights or take an active part in many of the festival's activities.

In a relaxed, Scandinavian atmosphere, dance, art, customs, music, and tasty food tidbits blend together to provide festival goers with an opportunity to experience and learn more about rich Nordic culture.

Expert cooks prepare exotic and delicious Scandinavian food delights including aebleskivers, krumkake, lefse, and rosettes. Food booths offer an assortment of mouth-watering favorites—pastries, meatballs, polse, and Swedish pancakes. This colorful day of flags, anthems, and traditional costumes culminates in an authentic smorgasbord that's guaranteed to please your palate.

California Lutheran University is located in Thousand Oaks, midway between Santa Barbara and Los Angeles.

POTATO LEFSE

4 cups potatoes

1 stick butter

salt to taste

2 cups flour

$^1/_2$ cup milk

Mash potatoes while still hot, immediately after boiling and draining. Add butter, and salt to taste. Cool overnight.

Mix potatoes, flour, and milk. Form into small balls. Roll balls out on a floured board or use a pie cloth and a covered roller (uses less flour). Bake on a hot griddle until light golden brown. Turn and bake on the other side. Remove and place on a cloth. Keep covered. Delicious served with butter and sugar.

Rozella Hagwen
Women's League of California Lutheran University

These potato lefses store well in the freezer.

DANISH COFFEE CAKE

For crust: Mix flour, butter, and water as if making pie crust. Roll on floured cloth into 2 long strips 3 inches wide and $^1/_4$-inch thick.

For filling: Mix butter and water, bring to a boil. Add vanilla. Remove from heat. Beat in flour by hand, stirring constantly so it won't lump. Stir in eggs vigorously by hand—one at a time. Spread over crusts almost to edges. Bake at 350° for 55 to 60 minutes. Cut in 1-inch diagonal strips to serve; sprinkle with powdered sugar for frosting and sliced almonds.

Women's League of California Lutheran University
Thousand Oaks

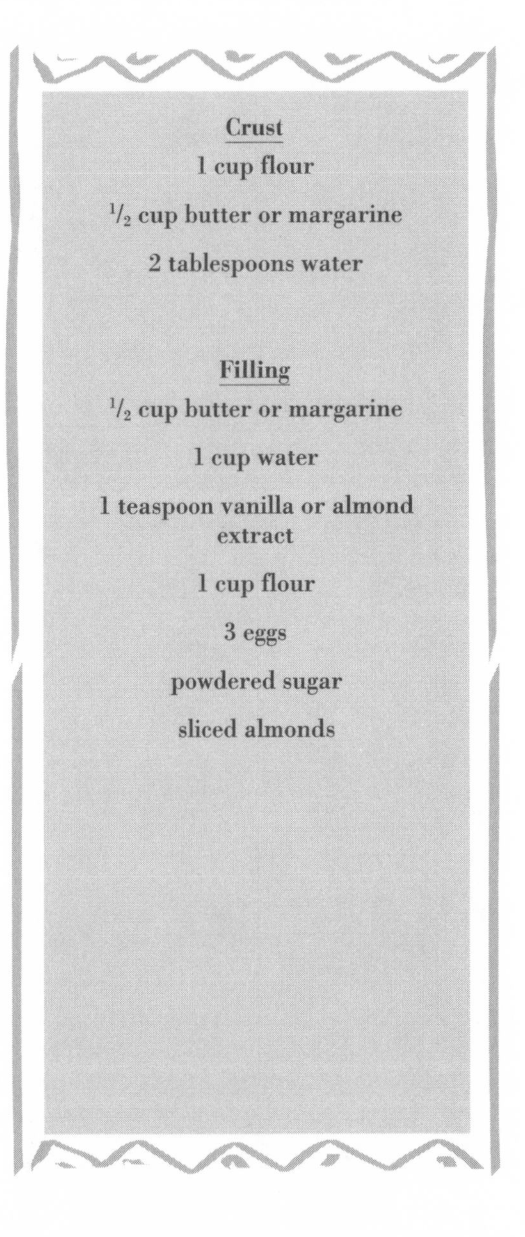

Crust

1 cup flour

$^1/_2$ cup butter or margarine

2 tablespoons water

Filling

$^1/_2$ cup butter or margarine

1 cup water

1 teaspoon vanilla or almond extract

1 cup flour

3 eggs

powdered sugar

sliced almonds

SIGNE ANDERSON'S SWEDISH BROWNIES

1 cup sugar

2 eggs

1¼ cups flour

½ cup margarine or butter, melted

1 teaspoon almond extract

⅓ cup chopped almonds

sugar

Heat oven to 350°. Combine sugar and eggs until well blended in medium bowl. Stir in flour, mix well. Add margarine and extract, stir until well mixed. Pour into greased 9-inch square baking pan. Sprinkle with almonds and sugar. Bake for 30 to 35 minutes or until lightly browned. Cut into bars while hot. Cool completely. Makes 30 bars. Sprinkle sparkles on top if desired.

Women's League of California Lutheran University
Thousand Oaks, CA

Notice that these moist, cake-like "blondies" contain no chocolate.

SOUPER 101 ROUNDUP

BUELLTON

Annual. Second weekend in October.

Everything's coming up super when Buellton holds its annual Souper 101 Roundup to celebrate a bountiful harvest. The entertainment includes arts and crafts booths, food and beverage booths, Kiddyland, a petting zoo, pony rides, and a rodeo that features both professional and amateur participants.

Saturday's parade is filled with regional bands, decorated floats, costumed locals, and more. The parade is full of surprises, and everyone who participates in the parade or observes from the curb has one heck of a time.

Throughout the weekend, live entertainment includes music, a youth symphony, Native American dances, ballet performances, and the toe-tapping sounds of old-time fiddlers.

Sunday activities include the farmers' market along Avenue of the Flags. You'll find plenty of local produce and products to whet your appetite. You'll want to check out the results of the Pea Soup Eating Contest. You can bring your own or taste one that's been provided. Both adults and youngsters compete for the best soup-eater title. Ostrich burgers are a rare and popular delicacy served at the roundup. The event's grand finale takes place at the R. T. Buell Arena, where local and professional riders perform during a Wild West show and rodeo.

Buellton is internationally known as the home of Pea Soup Andersen's. Since 1924, when Anton and Juliette Andersen first opened a tiny restaurant, travelers have stopped their journey long enough to take a break from driving, gas up their cars, and have a bite to eat in the famous eatery.

PEA SOUP ANDERSEN'S ORIGINAL RECIPE

2 cups Andersen's Selected Green Split Peas

2 quarts soft water

1 branch of celery, coarsely chopped

1 large carrot, chopped

1 small onion, chopped

1/4 teaspoon ground thyme

1 pinch cayenne

1 bay leaf

salt and pepper to taste

Combine all ingredients. Boil hard for 20 minutes, then slowly until peas are tender. Strain through fine sieve and reheat to boiling point. Makes 8 bowls of Andersen's Famous Split Pea Soup.

Pea Soup Andersen's (restaurant)
Buellton, CA

STIR-FRY OSTRICH AND TOMATO

In a mixing bowl, toss together meat, soy sauce, sake, salt, and white pepper. Set aside. Heat a large wok or heavy skillet to medium-high to high heat. Add peanut oil and heat until oil sizzles. Add ginger root, garlic, and red pepper flakes. Stir-fry 1 minute. Add reserved meat mixture, separating slices, and stir-fry 1 to 2 minutes. Do not overcook. Remove meat with a slotted spoon and set aside. Adding more oil if needed, stir-fry onion and sweet pepper until they begin to soften (about 2 minutes). Add tomatoes, cover, and heat until steam rises (about 5 minutes). Return meat to wok, add sesame oil, and stir to heat briefly. Serve immediately, garnished with cilantro sprigs.

Avilean Meats
Santa Ynez, CA

Serve over freshly steamed rice or crisp pan-fried Chinese noodles.

1 pound ostrich steak, thinly sliced on the diagonal across the grain

1 1/2 tablespoons soy sauce

1 1/2 tablespoon sake or dry sherry

1/2 teaspoon salt

1/4 teaspoon freshly ground white pepper

2 tablespoons peanut or corn oil

4 thin slices ginger root

4 garlic cloves, bruised

1/2 to 1 teaspoon red pepper flakes (optional)

1 yellow onion, cut into eighths and layers separated

1 green or red sweet pepper, cut into 1/2-inch squares

4 ripe tomatoes, each cut into eighths

1/2 to 1 teaspoon sesame oil

fresh cilantro sprigs

ESCAROLE, ORZO, AND GARBANZO SOUP MENOTTI

8 cups homemade chicken stock

½ cup orzo pasta (or pulcini)

1 cup garbanzo beans (chickpeas)

1 medium head escarole (1 pound), washed

freshly grated Parmesan cheese

black pepper to taste

Heat broth in a large stockpot and bring to a boil. Add pasta and reduce to low boil. Cook for 5 minutes and skim off foam. Add garbanzo beans and let cook for 4 to 5 minutes. Stack clean escarole leaves and chop into small pieces. Add to broth and cook, uncovered, at a gentle simmer for about 10 minutes. Serve with freshly grated Parmesan cheese and black pepper.

Chef Andy Lo Russo
Sing & Cook Italian cookbook
Santa Barbara, CA

CURES ANYTHING CHICKEN SOUP

In a saucepan, combine broth and 1 cup water. Bring to a boil. Stir in rice and boil for 15 minutes, or until tender. In a bowl, whisk together $^1/_4$ cup lemon juice and eggs. Whisk in 1 cup of the broth. Whisk the mixture into the remaining broth; add chicken. Cook over medium-low heat, whisking for 3 minutes or until chicken is tender and mixture is slightly thickened. Add salt, pepper, and remaining lemon juice to taste. Serve soup sprinkled with dill.

Bob Carter
Oxnard, CA

I'm not a doctor, but this soup, once served to me on a sickbed, is recommended for poor health, bad disposition, unsavory character, all loved ones, hot weather, cold weather, staying home, family outings, summer, winter, spring, fall, and just for the heck of it!

5 cups canned chicken broth

$^1/_4$ cup long grain rice

$^1/_3$ cup fresh lemon juice

3 large eggs

$^1/_2$ pound skinless, boneless chicken breast, cut into $^1/_4$-inch pieces

salt and pepper to taste

2 tablespoons snipped fresh dill

SQUID FESTIVAL

MONTEREY

Annual. Memorial Day weekend.

37

The Great Monterey Squid Festival is both a tribute to the commercial fishing industry of Monterey Bay and a succulent celebration of the incredible, edible squid. Thousands of pounds of savory squid, continuous family entertainment, and some unforgettable exhibits add up to a fun-filled festival weekend.

You'll be treated to a host of special exhibits focusing on the bay's commercial fishing industry, especially the squid catch, a major resource in the area. Microscopic squid eggs are displayed alongside giant, bathtub-size squid. The Squid Festival has something to offer for all ages. Other features include marine life, commercial fishing, cooking demonstrations, arts and crafts booths, and food booths serving squid in a variety of tempting ways.

One popular attraction at the festival is the demonstration showing how to clean and prepare squid for cooking. Chefs from local restaurants and hotels offer cooking demonstrations using their favorite recipes. The free entertainment schedule includes four separate stages, with one stage devoted entirely to children's acts. The other three stages feature all forms of musical entertainment.

Located 125 miles south of San Francisco and 345 miles north of Los Angeles, the Monterey Peninsula is formed by Monterey Bay to the north, the Pacific Ocean to the west, and Carmel Bay to the south.

BLACKENED CALAMARI PIZZA

- 1 pound pizza dough in a ball
- sprinkle of flour
- 2 tablespoons olive oil
- 2 cloves garlic, minced
- 1 cup marinara sauce
- 1½ cups shredded mozzarella cheese
- ½ each red, yellow, green peppers, sliced thin
- ¼ cup sliced black olives
- 1 ounce grated Romano cheese
- 1 ounce grated Parmesan cheese
- 2 tablespoons blackened spices for fish
- ½ pound fresh calamari, tenderized, sliced into ½-inch pieces
- 3 green onion bottoms, sliced

Preheat oven to 450°. Roll dough to a 12-inch round on a 12-inch pizza screen. Use flour on screen, and any utensils, to keep dough from sticking. Brush half of the olive oil and half of the garlic on flattened dough. Spread sauce on dough, leaving a ½-inch border on the edge. Add mozzarella cheese evenly to cover the sauce. Top with bell peppers and olives in an attractive pattern. Sprinkle pizza with Romano and Parmesan cheese and bake at 450° for 12 minutes or until crust is done. While pizza is cooking, mix blackened spices with calamari. Heat 1 tablespoon olive oil and garlic in skillet and sauté calamari for 1 minute. Remove pizza from oven and top with calamari. Top with green onions and extra Romano or Parmesan cheese if desired.

Pacific Coast Catering & Pizza
Valley Hills Center, Carmel Valley, CA
First Place Winner, Great Monterey Squid Festival

SQUID FIESTA

1 yellow onion, chopped

2 cloves garlic, minced

1/4 cup olive oil

1 large red pepper, cut in strips

1 large green pepper

2 medium zucchini, sliced

1/2 pound fresh mushrooms, sliced

1 15-ounce jar marinara sauce

1 8-ounce can tomato sauce

1/4 teaspoon sugar, optional

1 tablespoon water

1 cup red wine

1/8 teaspoon cinnamon

1/4 cup Parmesan cheese

1/2 teaspoon oregano

2 pounds squid, cleaned and tenderized, cut into pieces

flour and water to thicken sauce

salt and pepper to taste

In large frying pan, sauté onion and garlic in olive oil until onion is translucent. Add red and green peppers, zucchini, and mushrooms; cook 3 minutes. Add marinara sauce and tomato sauce, sugar, and 1 cup water. Cook a few minutes longer. Add wine, cinnamon, Parmesan cheese, and oregano. Cook 10 minutes over medium heat, stirring often. Add squid, cover, and simmer 20 minutes. Mix flour and water and add to dish to thicken sauce; salt and pepper to taste.

Serve with garlic bread and salad if desired.

Great Monterey Squid Festival Cookbook
Monterey, CA

VEGETABLE-STUFFED SQUID RINGS

Cook whole mantles in boiling salted water for 1 hour or until tender; drain. Sauté carrots and onion in oil for 5 minutes, stirring occasionally. Add tomato and catsup, cook additional 5 minutes. Season with salt and pepper. Cut mantles into wide rings. Stuff rings with vegetable mixture. Chill before serving.

Great Monterey Squid Festival Cookbook
Monterey, CA

1½ pounds whole squid mantles

3 medium carrots, finely grated

1 small onion, finely chopped

4 tablespoons oil

1 large tomato, peeled, finely chopped

2 tablespoons catsup

salt and pepper to taste

CALAMARI RISOTTO

2 to 3 pounds whole squid mantles
2 tablespoons olive oil
2 cloves garlic, crushed
1 cup water
1/2 cup dry white wine
2 tablespoons tomato paste
1/3 cup chopped black olives
1/8 teaspoon red pepper
salt and black pepper to taste

Cut mantles into 1/4-inch rings. Sauté squid and garlic in hot oil until brown. Add water, wine, tomato paste, and olives. Season with peppers and salt. Cover and cook 45 minutes or until squid is tender. Serve on rice.

Great Monterey Squid Festival Cookbook
Monterey, CA

STRAWBERRY FESTIVAL

OXNARD

Annual. Third weekend in May.

Oxnard produces 23 percent of the total California strawberry crop, shipping more than 120,000 tons annually. It's no wonder people go bananas over strawberries each year at the California Strawberry Festival.

As you drive into the community, you'll see it's surrounded by huge strawberry fields. Bright red strawberry flags fly from berry-laden produce stands. It's the perfect setting for one of the nation's top outdoor festivals.

Festival goers have their pick of gourmet dishes, and you'll want to try them all. There are strawberry crepes and blintzes, strawberry muffins and bread, strawberry cheesecake on a stick, strawberry shortcake, chocolate-dipped strawberries, strawberry beverages, and more.

Each year, festival organizers sponsor the Berry-Off, a national strawberry cooking competition. It's held as a prelude to the festival. The contest draws hundreds of original entries from across the country, and three finalists are invited to prepare their dishes at the Battle of the Berries.

If you're the adventurous type, go ahead and have your pie-in-the-face by participating in the Strawberry Shortcake Eating Contest or the Strawberry Tart

(Continued)

Toss. Afterwards, you'll want to cheer on the waiters and waitresses as restaurant personnel traverse an obstacle course toting trays of strawberries, shortcake, and wine.

More than two hundred booths of "berried" treasures are on display and for sale during the Fine Arts & Crafts Show. You'll get a chance to visit with artists and crafts-people as they demonstrate and exhibit their work.

A special place called Strawberryland is dedicated to young festival goers. It's filled with an array of children's activities and musical performances. Strawberry-loving kids enjoy magic and variety acts, have the opportunity to ride the Strawberry Express, learn about animals in the petting zoo, and play with strawberry-scented play dough in the hands-on arts and crafts tent.

To round out the weekend's events, fitness-oriented individuals and families can partake in Sunday's 10K race and 2-mile family fun run along the beautiful Pacific Ocean shoreline. Performing artists bring an array of musical styles to the festival and entertain on three festival stages. Nationally renowned headliners perform at the Strawberry Meadows Amphitheater, a permanent concert venue at the event site.

The coastal community of Oxnard is located off U.S. Highway 101 and California Highway 1, between Malibu and Santa Barbara.

STRAWBERRY-MANGO SALSA

1 pint ripe strawberries, cleaned, hulled, chopped

1 ripe mango, peeled, chopped

1 Habeñero chili, seeded, finely chopped

3 jalapeño chilies, seeded, finely chopped

4 serrano chilies, seeded, finely chopped

½ medium red onion, chopped

3 tablespoons chopped cilantro

Mix all ingredients in small bowl.

Shaunna K. Zavala
First Place Winner, Hors d'Oeurves division
Ventura, CA

Excellent for chip dipping, or as a condiment on broiled fish.

MEDITERRANEAN STRAWBERRY LUNCH SALAD

Salad Dressing

1/4 cup light olive oil

1/4 cup balsamic vinegar

1/2 teaspoon Dijon mustard

Salad Ingredients

4 cups mixed greens, washed, chilled

2 cups fresh strawberries, cleaned, halved

2 large naval oranges, peeled, sliced in quarters

1 cup seedless green grapes, rinsed, dried

1/2 cup coarsely chopped walnuts

1/2 cup salad dressing, divided

1/4 pound gorgonzola cheese, crumbled

To prepare dressing, combine all ingredients in blender or with whisk. Makes about 1/2 cup. Set aside in refrigerator.

Prepare salad greens and refrigerate until needed. Toss strawberries, oranges, grapes, and walnuts with 2 tablespoons salad dressing. Toss salad greens with remainder of dressing. Place greens on individual plates. Mound fruit-walnut mixture on top of greens. Sprinkle with gorgonzola cheese. Serve with fresh Italian bread.

Carmen Collins
Metuchen, New Jersey
First Place Winner, Soups and Salads division

SPICED STRAWBERRY RELISH

In a large, heavy saucepan, bring wine, vinegar, brown sugar, granulated sugar, and lemon juice just to a boil over medium-high heat. Reduce heat to medium and stir for 2 minutes. Add remaining ingredients and simmer uncovered over medium-low heat for 1 hour, stirring occasionally. Place mixture in a glass container and cool completely.

Serve chilled or at room temperature over ham steak or poultry.

Stuart Byford
Waldron, Arkansas
Grand Prize Winner

- 1/2 cup red wine
- 1/2 cup red wine vinegar
- 1/2 cup firmly packed brown sugar
- 1/3 cup granulated sugar
- 1/8 cup fresh lemon juice
- 1 teaspoon freshly grated lemon zest
- 1 teaspoon finely chopped ginger root
- 1/4 teaspoon ground cinnamon
- 1/4 teaspoon ground cloves
- 1/4 teaspoon ground allspice
- 1/2 cup coarsely chopped, peeled peach
- 1/2 cup coarsely chopped, peeled pear
- 2 1/2 cups coarsely chopped fresh strawberries
- 1/4 cup chopped onion

LUSCIOUS BERRY TRIFLE

6 cups sliced fresh strawberries

4 cups cubed cantaloupe

2 cups sliced kiwi

1/2 cup strawberry all-fruit spread

2 8-ounce packages fat-free cream cheese, softened

1 1/2 cups confectioner's sugar

1 cup fat-free sour cream

2 cups frozen light whipped topping, thawed

1 10 1/2-ounce loaf angel food cake, cubed

1/2 cup grated semisweet chocolate

1 whole strawberry, sliced decoratively for garnish

In a large bowl, toss strawberries, cantaloupe, and kiwi with strawberry fruit spread. Set aside.

In a medium mixing bowl, beat the cream cheese and confectioner's sugar until smooth. Add the sour cream, mix well. Fold in whipped topping and cake. Drain juice from fruit mixture. In a trifle dish or deep salad bowl, layer 1/3 of fruit, 1/3 of cake mixture, and 1/3 of chocolate. Repeat layers twice. Garnish with sliced strawberry.

Paula Marchese
Rocky Point, Long Island, New York
First Place Winner, Desserts division

STRAWBERRY FESTIVAL

SANTA MARIA

Annual. Fourth weekend in April.

It's the mild winters and cool summers that help growers in the Santa Maria Valley produce some of the state's tastiest strawberries. The annual Strawberry Festival highlights the beginning of the strawberry season and the importance of the strawberry industry to the local economy.

As you'd expect, desserts are plentiful and include everything strawberry fresh and savory—from plain to chocolate-dipped. You'll find plenty of variety as you wander the festival grounds and select succulent, freshly picked berries. A farmers' market, cook-off, and tasting pavilion highlight the local produce and especially the berry. Plan to arrive hungry! Local cooks produce a menu that offers berries, berries, and more berries.

In addition to eating, you'll want to visit the Strawberry Fields Forever art show, take part in pie-eating contests, join in during the Berry Bingo Bash, and observe plenty of games, crafts, and berry-related educational activities.

In keeping with festival tradition, an expansive carnival, complete with a Berry-Go-Round, provides youngsters of all ages an opportunity to enjoy games, clowns, interactive exhibits, outdoor musical entertainment, and a craft fair where kids make art from all kinds of scrap materials. Kid's Place offers children a soap bubble challenge, a strawberry pie eating contest, pony rides, and a petting zoo.

(Continued)

A special feature of each year's festival is the annual harvest competition among area agricultural workers. The competition judges workers on speed, berry packaging presentation, and the grooming and care of plants. The contest is held prior to the festival, and awards are presented during the festival weekend. The farm worker competition is the only event of its kind in the state that's held in conjunction with a community festival.

This very berry weekend of events takes place at the beautiful Santa Barbara County Fairgrounds, in Santa Maria.

STRAWBERRY-CHOCOLATE GERMAN PANCAKE

Preheat oven to 425°. Melt butter in 10-inch ovenproof skillet. In electric blender, combine eggs, milk and flour; blend until smooth. Pour into hot skillet. Bake 2 minutes. Remove from oven; sprinkle chocolate pieces over pancake and return to oven. Bake 15 to 20 minutes until puffed and golden brown. Top with strawberries and dust with sugar. Cut into wedges and serve immediately . . . as if you could wait!

California Strawberry Advisory Board
Watsonville, CA

For dessert, this crisp, baked pancake makes a perfect strawberry bowl.

1/4 cup butter or margarine

4 eggs

1 cup milk

1 cup flour

powered sugar

1 cup semisweet chocolate pieces

1 pint fresh strawberries, stemmed, sliced

CLASSIC STRAWBERRY SHORTCAKE

2 cups flour

1/4 cup sugar

4 teaspoons baking powder

1/4 teaspoon salt

dash nutmeg

1/2 cup butter or margarine

1/2 cup milk

2 eggs, separated

additional sugar

2 pints fresh strawberries, stemmed, sliced

1 cup whipping cream, whipped and sweetened

Sift flour, sugar, baking powder, salt, and nutmeg into large bowl. Cut in butter to resemble coarse meal. In bowl, blend milk and egg yolks with fork. Stir into flour mixture to make a soft dough. Divide dough into 6 portions, form into balls. Pat balls out on greased baking sheet to 3-inch circles, moistening fingers with egg whites. Brush cakes with egg whites. Sprinkle with sugar. Bake in preheated 450° oven 10 to 12 minutes until golden. Remove to rack, cool. Sweeten strawberries to taste. Halve cakes horizontally. On plates, fill and garnish with strawberries and whipped cream.

California Strawberry Advisory Board
Watsonville, CA

HONEY-ALMOND STRAWBERRY DIP

Rinse strawberries and pat dry with paper towels, set aside. Whisk remaining ingredients together until smooth. Serve in small bowl to accompany strawberries.

California Strawberry Advisory Board
Watsonville, CA

2 pint baskets fresh strawberries

$^{2}/_{3}$ cup nonfat yogurt

3 tablespoons finely chopped, toasted, slivered almonds

$2^{1}/_{2}$ tablespoons honey

STRAWBERRY CREAM DIP

2 pint baskets fresh strawberries

1/2 cup light sour cream

1/4 cup strawberry fruit spread or strawberry jam

Rinse strawberries and pat dry with paper towels; set aside. Whisk remaining ingredients together until smooth. Serve in small bowl to accompany strawberries.

California Strawberry Advisory Board
Watsonville, CA

SUMMER FARMERS MARKET

CORONADO

Annual. One weekend a month, May-October.

We've all been to farmers' markets, right? Let me warn you, this one is like no other. First, it is held in one of southern California's most magnificent coastal settings. In addition, the offerings include many of the region's top farmers' produce, gourmet foods, cooking classes, and tastings featuring food by chefs and cookbook authors. Don't miss trying the tasty barbecued ribs and fresh-roasted corn.

As local growers display and sell their bounty, you'll discover a wonderful variety of top-quality produce: mushrooms, specialty beans, lettuces, herbs, raspberries, citrus, papaya, mangos, tomatoes, artichokes, squash, white corn, and strawberries.

At each market, complimentary cooking demonstrations and tastings feature national and local culinary professionals. Many of the participants have won international culinary awards.

This very special farmers' market is held at the luxurious Loews Coronado Bay Resort, one of America's most exquisite ports of call.

(Continued)

Trust me. After visiting the resort, strolling through impeccable grounds, feasting in award-winning restaurants, watching demonstrations by outstanding chefs, and discovering high-quality produce, you'll think you've found the ultimate farmers' market paradise.

Coronado is one of San Diego's resort destinations. To get to the peninsula community, cross over the dramatic 2.3-mile San Diego-Coronado Bridge, and you're on the enchanted island.

All of the recipes in the Summer Farmers Market section are from Executive Chef James Boyce, Loews Coronado Bay Resort.

LOEWS CORONADO BAY RESORT'S MEMORIAL DAY BARBECUE SAUCE

Cut and combine all peppers and garlic. Heat oil over medium heat in thick-bottomed skillet. Cook peppers until golden brown. Add remaining ingredients and simmer until peppers are tender. Remove from heat and blend thoroughly.

This spicy barbecue sauce is splendid on grilled meats and poultry.

2 Anaheim peppers

1 medium green pepper

4 cloves garlic

2 dried Ancho chilies

2 teaspoons crushed red peppers

2 tablespoons olive oil

2 cups chili sauce

2 tablespoons Dijon mustard

$^1/_4$ cup soy sauce

$^1/_2$ cup orange juice concentrate

CREAM OF PUMPKIN SOUP WITH HERBS

1 tablespoon butter

1 small onion, peeled and chopped

1 small pumpkin ($2^1/_2$ pounds) peeled, seeded, cut into large pieces

4 cups chicken broth

4 cups heavy cream

2 teaspoons sugar

freshly ground nutmeg to taste

salt and pepper to taste

$^1/_2$ cup fresh herbs (parsley, chives, tarragon), chopped

Place butter in medium saucepan over medium heat. Add onion and pumpkin, cook slowly for 5 minutes; do not allow any browning. Add chicken broth and simmer for 20 minutes. Remove from heat, add heavy cream and sugar. Place in blender and purée until smooth. Adjust seasonings, salt, pepper, and nutmeg. Garnish with chopped herbs.

In a hurry? This rich, creamy pumpkin soup can be prepared in less than 30 minutes.

TOMATO, CUCUMBER AND RED ONION RELISH

Peel and seed cucumber. Slice diagonally 1/4 inch thick. Slice red onion into 1/4-inch slices. Cut tomatoes into 4 pieces. Finely chop pepper. Mix all ingredients in a medium-size mixing bowl and refrigerate for half an hour before serving. Season to taste.

1 European cucumber

1 medium red onion

3 vine-ripened plum tomatoes

1 small jalapeño pepper

1/2 cup aged red wine vinegar

2 tablespoons chopped mint

salt and pepper to taste

SWEDISH FESTIVAL

KINGSBURG

Annual. Thursday-Sunday, third weekend in May.

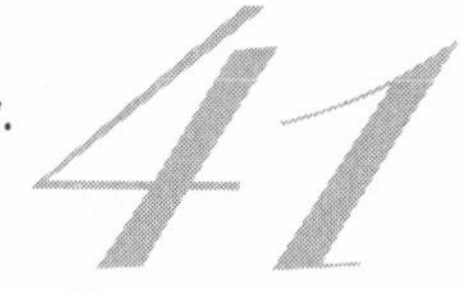

One of Kingsburg's biggest attractions is the colorful Swedish Festival. To get you into a feasting mood, the festival offers Swedish pancake breakfasts, pancake suppers, and enough sausage, lingonberries, boysenberries, and smorgasbord to give you a sugar high and a satisfied palate.

Prior to the weekend festivities, the Swedish practice of serving pea soup and pancakes on Thursday is honored in an evening feast. On this occasion, the Swedish Festival Queen is crowned amid much merriment and plenty of entertainment.

Friday, the huge community smorgasbord features foods from the different provinces of Sweden. You can't miss the event, which takes place in the downtown "coffee pot" park. Afterwards, the local Kiwanis Club sponsors travelogues showing Sweden, Norway, and Denmark. It's like traveling to Europe without leaving California.

You can get actively into the swing of things by dancing around the maypole to the sounds of Swedish music and participating in the Dala Horse Trot. Or, what about cheering on the bands, floats, and drill teams at Saturday's festival parade?

A wide variety of arts, crafts, and food booths are the keystones of this event. There are cultural demonstrations, live entertainment, dancing instructions, and an opportunity to learn more about Swedish culture at the Kingsburg Museum.

The central California city of Kingsburg, with its shingled roofs, gables, dormer windows, and cross-boarded architecture, continues to reflect its Swedish heritage. You'll know you're there when you see the distinctive Coffee Pot Water tower looming over the village. It's your "Välkommen to Kingsburg" greeting. All recipes were contributed by Kingsburg Swedish Festival.

SWEDISH MEATBALLS

Sauté onion in 1 tablespoon butter. Mix crumbs, water, and seasonings, and mix well with meat. Shape into small balls and cook in remaining butter, browning well. Shake pan continuously to make balls round. Serve with boiled potatoes, pan-gravy, pickled cucumbers, and lingonberries.

1 tablespoon finely chopped onion

2 to 3 tablespoons butter

1/3 cup bread crumbs

1 cup water

1 1/2 teaspoons salt

1/2 teaspoon pepper

1 pound ground beef

PICKLED CUCUMBERS

4 cucumbers, very thinly sliced

1/2 cup vinegar

1 1/2 cups water

1 teaspoon salt

1/2 teaspoon white pepper

1 to 2 tablespoons chopped parsley

Mix all ingredients and refrigerate for at least 1 hour before serving.

SWEDISH PANCAKES

Mix flour, milk, and salt. Add eggs one at a time. Fry in margarine. Serve with lingonberry jam.

To make lunch filling: Melt margarine, add flour, and stir. Pour in milk a little at a time, stirring constantly to avoid lumps. Add chicken and mushrooms. Season to taste. Divide the filling among the pancakes, roll them, and put in an ovenproof dish or platter. Put 3 to 5 pats of butter on top. Sprinkle with bread crumbs and Parmesan cheese. Put in oven at 350° for 15 to 20 minutes or until heated. Serve with lettuce, avocado, and grapefruit sections with Thousand Island dressing.

1 cup flour

2 cups milk

1/4 teaspoon salt

2 eggs

2 to 3 tablespoons margarine

(If for dessert add
1/4 tablespoon sugar)

For Lunch Filling

3 tablespoons margarine

3 tablespoons flour

1 cup milk

2 5-ounce cans boned chicken with juice

1 can mushroom pieces with juice

1/8 teaspoon white pepper

1/8 teaspoon salt

3 to 5 pats of butter

bread crumbs

Parmesan cheese

TASTE OF SOLVANG

SOLVANG

Annual. Mid-March weekend.

42

Close your eyes and imagine a warm family kitchen, the smell of rich pastry, and the taste of tarts, cheese rolls, and apple brown Betty. You're apt to discover it all as Solvang celebrates its famous taste treats during the Taste of Solvang. During the event, the storybook village comes alive with Danish-style entertainment, colorful flags and costumes, and the aroma of national and international cuisine.

The festive weekend kicks off Friday evening, when you'll get a chance to experience a ballroom full of scrumptious desserts and live entertainment. You won't want to miss being one of the first to enjoy this glittering night of rich music. During the two-hour Dessert Showcase some of Solvang's finest chefs and cooks tempt you with their masterful creations. Go ahead . . . indulge in your own dessert fantasies.

Saturday you may be in the perfect mood to walk off some of Friday night's desserts. If so, the Walking Smorgasbord is just what you're looking for. It's your chance to journey through the entire village while sampling a variety of dazzling Danish food and entertainment in an old-world atmosphere. Many of the town's restaurants, bakeries, candy stores, and gourmet food stores open their doors and welcome you. If you'd rather ride than walk, hop aboard the charming and authentic turn-of-the-century trolley. Pulled by two Belgian horses, the streetcar will transport you around town in style.

Just in case you didn't get enough to eat during the first two days, on Sunday you're invited to sample a bit of the world's largest Danish. It, along with dancers and musicians, brings the feasting to a fitting close.

A word of warning: this popular taste-fest sells out quickly. Festival organizers suggest you make your plans early in the year in order to avoid disappointment. All tastings held during this rain-or-shine event require a festival pass, available for advance purchase at the Solvang Conference & Visitors Bureau.

ÆBLESKIVER

3 eggs

2 cups buttermilk

1 teaspoon sugar

*1/2 teaspoon salt

*2 cups flour

*1 tablespoon baking powder

*1 teaspoon baking soda

1/4 teaspoon cardamom

(*2 cups biscuit mix may be used for starred ingredients)

Separate the eggs; beat yolks and add buttermilk, sugar, and salt. Sift together and add flour, baking powder, soda, and cardamom. Fold in stiffly beaten egg whites. Heat æbleskiver pan. Put 1 teaspoon oil in each hole and fill completely with batter. Cook until slightly crusty on bottom. Turn slightly with a knitting needle or skewer. Continue cooking, turning the ball to keep it from burning, until the knitting needle comes out clean when stuck in the center. Serve hot with jam and powdered sugar.

Solvang Conference & Visitors Bureau
Solvang, CA

Æbleskiver is a pancake-like batter cooked in special pans that turn out little round treats described as the Danish version of doughnuts. Æbleskivers are served year-round in many Solvang restaurants. Special pans may be purchased in many Solvang stores.

DANISH RICE PUDDING

2 8-ounce packages nonfat cream cheese, softened

$^2/_3$ cup confectioner's sugar

$^1/_4$ cup milk

3 cups cooked rice, cooled

$^1/_3$ cup slivered almonds, toasted

1 teaspoon vanilla extract

1 8-ounce container nondairy whipped topping, thawed

1 20-ounce can cherry pie filling

Beat cream cheese, sugar, and milk in large bowl. Stir in rice, almonds, and vanilla. Fold in whipped topping. Top each serving with 2 tablespoons cherry pie filling.

U.S.A. Rice Council
Houston, TX

GRILLED PACIFIC SALMON WITH TABOULEH AND PAPAYA

mixed baby greens

lemon and olive oil vinaigrette (see recipe next page)

6 salmon steaks, seasoned and grilled

1 pound tabouleh salad (see recipe next page)

2 ripe papayas, peeled, sliced

1 cucumber, sliced

2 vine-ripened tomatoes, quartered

1 grilled Maui onion, sliced

black sesame seeds

chopped parsley

Mix baby greens with lemon and olive oil vinaigrette and place in center of large platter. Arrange grilled salmon and tabouleh around greens. Decorate plate with papaya, cucumber, tomato, and grilled Maui onion. Sprinkle with black sesame seeds and chopped parsley.

Chef Pascal Godé
Alisal Ranch
Solvang, CA

TABOULEH SALAD

3/4 cup medium-grain bulgur

1 bunch flat leaf parsley, finely chopped

1/2 bunch fresh mint, leaves only, chopped fine

1 bunch scallions, thinly sliced

3 tomatoes, diced

juice of 1 lemon

1/2 cup olive oil

salt and pepper to taste

Lemon and Olive Oil Vinaigrette

1/3 cup lemon juice

1 cup olive oil

salt and pepper to taste

6 leaves basil, chopped

2 cloves garlic, chopped

For salad: In a bowl, cover bulgur with fresh cold water to a depth of about 1 inch. Set aside to soak for 20 to 30 minutes while you chop and dice the vegetables. When bulgur grains are nicely plump, drain them, squeezing out as much water as you can (turn the grains onto a clean kitchen towel and squeeze out the remaining water). Each grain of bulgur should be moist and plump without a trace of liquid.

Pour bulgur into a dry bowl, add all the chopped and diced vegetables. Mix well with your hands, squeezing slightly to release the flavors. When well mixed, squeeze the lemon juice over it, add oil, and toss to blend together. Season with salt and pepper, additional lemon juice, and oil as desired.

For dressing: mix all ingredients together.

Chef Pascal Godé
Alisal Ranch
Solvang, CA

TASTE OF VENTURA COUNTY

VENTURA COUNTY

Annual. Last weekend in April.

43

There's nothing quite like warm spring sun, soft breezes, salt air, family, friends, food, and fun. That's what you'll discover as many of Ventura County's favorite chefs prepare their bills of fare during the annual Taste of Ventura County celebration.

Beginning Friday evening, A Taste of Ventura County provides fun-filled days of diverse offerings of food, wine, and entertainment. The celebrating takes place waterside, at Ventura County's Channel Islands Harbor in Oxnard.

Epicurean delights are offered by a variety of restaurants, and appetizer-size portions allow festival goers the chance to sample many selections, from simple to extravagant. You're apt to find choices such as grilled ostrich sausage, bruschetta, barbecued shrimp, clam chowder, chimichangas, and pizza. Dessert items range from chocolate-dipped strawberries to flan and iced mochas. Beverages run the gamut from beer-on-tap to frosty margaritas.

Shaded cafe tables, colorfully decorated booths, and a panoramic view of ships in the harbor add a unique ambiance to the waterside venue. Musical entertainment ranges from jazz, blues, and classic rock to swing and big-band sounds. If you want to dance, the dance floor provides you with just the right amount of footage.

You'll discover that fun and games for all ages are part of this festival. Adults vie for cash and prizes in the bingo tent while the children's area invites youngsters to partake in arts and crafts, face painting, science projects, and more. Firemen are usually on hand to let the kids climb aboard a vintage fire truck, complete with working lights and siren.

Sunday's Big Band Bash is always a special treat. You're able to get in step and swing dance, delight in the sounds of the golden era, savor an abundance of taste treats, and sample the champagnes that flow at discounted prices from 11 A.M. to 3 P.M.

To reach the Channel Islands Harbor, Oxnard, take U.S. Highway 101 to Victoria. Head south to Channel Islands Boulevard, turn right over the bridge to Harbor Boulevard, and follow the festival signs.

CAPISTRANO'S BRUSCHETTA

9 medium ripe tomatoes

2 tablespoons chopped fresh basil

$1^1/_2$ tablespoons finely minced fresh garlic

1 tablespoon virgin olive oil

1 tablespoon balsamic vinegar

$^1/_2$ tablespoon salt and pepper to taste

pinch of ground white pepper

Cut out the stem end of each tomato and cut an "x" on the opposite end. Now place the tomatoes in low-boiling water, for about 1 minute until the skins start to separate from the meat; remove from the water and immediately immerse in ice water. Do not overcook; you want the tomatoes to stay firm. After the tomatoes are cool, remove the skins, cut tomatoes in half crosswise and squeeze out the seeds. Then cut the tomatoes in a medium dice. Combine with remaining ingredients and refrigerate for 2 hours. Serve atop Capistrano's crostini (recipe follows).

Jean-Claude Guerin
Capistrano's Retaurant
Oxnard, CA

This "popular, easy-to-prepare dish is great in taste, great in simplicity, and great for your health."

CROSTINI

Cut baguette into slices about 1/4 inch thick and place them on a cookie sheet. Brush with butter or oil. Combine remaining ingredients and sprinkle evenly on all of the slices of bread. Bake in oven at 350° approximately 5 to 8 minutes or until crisp—but not burned. Remove from the oven and let cool. Place in a basket and serve.

Jean-Claude Guerin
Capistrano's Restaurant
Oxnard, CA

1 thin sourdough baguette (preferably 1 to 2 days old)

1/2 cup melted butter or olive oil

1/2 cup grated Parmesan cheese

1/2 teaspoon ground rosemary

1/2 teaspoon ground oregano

1/2 teaspoon paprika

1/2 teaspoon thyme leaves

NONA'S RISOTTO

Step One Ingredients

1 cup Arborio rice

2 tablespoons olive oil

2 cloves garlic, minced

$^1/_2$ red onion, chopped

$2^1/_2$ cups hot vegetable stock

Step Two Ingredients

2 tablespoons olive oil

meat and vegetable risotto mixture of your choice (see below)

1 clove garlic, minced

1 shallot, minced

fresh herbs

heavy cream

salt and freshly ground black pepper to taste

$^1/_2$ cup grated Parmesan cheese

Suggested Risotto Mixtures

*scallops, leeks, snow peas, sweet red peppers, and fresh dill.

*smoked salmon, red onion, red and green bell peppers, snow peas, and fresh dill.

*Italian sausage, sweet peas, red onion, red and green bell peppers, roasted garlic cloves, and fresh basil.

*ham, leeks, mushrooms, roasted garlic cloves, zucchini, and fresh rosemary.

Step one instructions: Sauté rice in olive oil with garlic and onion until rice is thoroughly coated with oil and onion is softened. Then begin adding hot stock, $^1/_2$ cup at a time, stirring frequently, until rice is al dente. This risotto base may now be covered and refrigerated for 2 or 3 days, if desired.

Step two instructions: Heat oil in a large sauté pan, add chopped meat and vegetables from the desired risotto mixture. Stir in minced garlic, shallot, and a healthy quantity of fresh herbs. Sauté until 90 percent cooked, then cover with heavy cream and reduce until the cream is slightly thickened.

Add the risotto base and sauté until the mixture is rich and creamy. Season to taste with salt and black pepper. Just before serving, stir in $^1/_2$ cup freshly grated Parmesan cheese.

Serve immediately, sprinkled with more Parmesan cheese and a small scoop of bruschetta.

Jonathan Enabnit, Food and Beverage Director
Nona's Courtyard Cafe, Bella Maggiore Inn
Ventura, CA

CEVICHE

In a large bowl, combine lemon and lime juices. Then add white pepper, salt, garlic, Tabasco, and salad oil. Mix well. Add the cubed red snapper, onions, cilantro, and bell pepper. Gently mix well. Refrigerate for 12 hours to blend flavors before serving. Serve 6 ounces of chilled ceviche on a bed of lettuce with a garnish of fresh lemon slices and a side dish of salsa.

Chef Jaime Ballesteros
Whale's Tail (restaurant)
Oxnard, CA

- 2½ cups lemon juice
- 1½ cups lime juice
- 1 tablespoon white pepper
- 1 tablespoon salt
- 1 tablespoon granulated garlic
- 1 ounce Tabasco sauce
- 2 ounces salad oil or canola oil
- 5 pounds Pacific red snapper, cut into ½-inch cubes
- ½ bunch green onions or scallions, diced
- ½ bunch fresh cilantro, chopped
- 1 medium bell pepper, diced

CAYENNE CHILI SALSA

2 cups canned diced tomatoes

1 cup diced yellow onion

1 cup diced red onion

1 cup diced green onion with tops

2 cups finely chopped cilantro

1 cup canned tomato sauce

2 tablespoons crushed Mexican oregano

1 tablespoon fine cumin

4 red, ripe cayenne peppers, stems removed, extremely finely chopped

6 ounces Trappeys Red Devil Cayenne Pepper Sauce

1/4 cup fresh lemon juice

Combine all ingredients in large bowl and mix well by hand. Place in covered container and let sit in refrigerator overnight. This salsa can be used anywhere you like to use salsa, but it is extremely good on any fish dish.

Chef Terry Foster
Smith & Smith
Ventura, CA

TOURNAMENT OF ROSES/ ROSE BOWL GAME

PASADENA

Annual. January 1.

44

On years that January 1 is a Sunday, parade and game are held on January 2.

No other California celebration is as well known and popular as the annual Tournament of Roses and Rose Bowl Game. Each year more than one million cheering spectators line the parade route, and another 450 million people see the parade and game on television. There's literally nothing in the world quite like the excitement, beauty, and spectacle of these major holiday events.

Many people camp overnight along the parade route, and you may want to begin the festivities by joining them. Otherwise, improve your chances by arriving early to find parking and viewing spaces. The parade begins promptly at 8:02 A.M. and lasts approximately two hours at any given point along the 5.5-mile route.

The game kicks off at 1:50 P.M. in the Rose Bowl Stadium. The stadium now has a seating capacity of 104,594 people. Believe me, there's not a vacant seat in the entire place.

Prior to the parade, you can watch the floats being decorated at several locations scattered throughout the city. You'll be fascinated as you watch the floats taking shape one petal and one seed at a time. Thousands of volunteers and employees

(Continued)

work for several days getting the floats decorated. After the parade, the floats can be seen up-close and personal in a display at the end of the parade route.

A word of caution: plan early. Hotel accommodations for this special celebration are often booked a year in advance.

MENU FOR TOURNAMENT OF ROSES/ROSE BOWL GAME PICNIC

(recipes follow)

Make your New Year's Day visit extra special by planning a tailgate picnic after the parade or before the game. What follows will keep you pleasantly feasting as you enjoy the special ambience of this annual event. The following menu and recipes were created as a Tournament of Roses and Rose Bowl game picnic by Anita Delfs, U.C.L.A. football fan and tailgate picnic lover. She recommends you prepare the picnic the day before and transport it in a cooler.

$^1/_2$ roasted Cornish game hen (per person)

artichoke with mayonnaise-mustard sauce (per person)

macaroni salad

baguette of French bread with butter

radish roses

apple turnover from local bakery

Rosé wine, lemonade, tea, or coffee

CORNISH GAME HENS

Remove giblet package and wash hen; pat dry with a paper towel. Cut hen in half. Season with salt and pepper, place on a rack in a flat roasting pan, skin side up. Brush each $^1/_2$ hen with melted butter. Roast uncovered at 375° for 50 minutes in a preheated oven. Remove from oven and cool. Wrap each $^1/_2$ hen in plastic wrap when completely cooled. Refrigerate and serve cold.

Cornish game hen
(plan $^1/_2$ hen per person)

salt and pepper

melted butter

ARTICHOKES

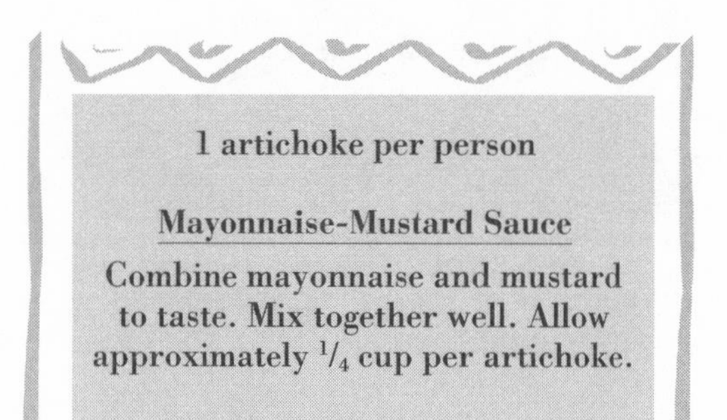

1 artichoke per person

Mayonnaise-Mustard Sauce

Combine mayonnaise and mustard to taste. Mix together well. Allow approximately 1/4 cup per artichoke.

Rinse each artichoke with cold water. Make a flat cut at the base so artichoke will sit flat. Using scissors, trim the tip off each leaf, removing the sharp sticker point. Place artichokes on a rack in a saucepan or pressure cooker.

#1 method: In saucepan with 1-inch of water, boil for approximately 1 hour or until the center/stem area is easily pierced with a fork. Do not allow pan to go dry.

#2 method: In pressure cooker with 1/2 inch water bring pressure cooker up to pressure, adjust fire, and cook for approximately 15 minutes for large artichokes.

Drain and cool, wrap individually in plastic wrap when completely cooled. Refrigerate and serve cold.

Artichoke leaves are delicious when dipped in Mayonnaise-Mustard Sauce.

MACARONI SALAD

Combine all ingredients in large bowl. Mix gently, cover, and allow flavors to "marry" in the refrigerator for 6 hours prior to serving.

8 ounces salad macaroni, cooked as instructed on package

$^{1}/_{2}$ cup chopped celery

$^{1}/_{4}$ cup chopped onion

$^{1}/_{4}$ cup chopped sweet pickle

1 cup high-quality mayonnaise

1 tablespoon mustard

1 teaspoon salt

$^{1}/_{8}$ teaspoon pepper

$^{1}/_{2}$ teaspoon Worcestershire sauce

2 dashes Tabasco sauce

1 2-ounce jar of chopped pimentos, drained

1 $2^{1}/_{4}$-ounce can of sliced black olives, drained

RADISH ROSES

12 medium-large, round, bright red radishes

Radishes may be cut to resemble roses. Cut the outside layer down from the tip toward the stem end in 5 or 6 thin sections, making the outside red covering stand out like petals. Place cut radishes in ice water for about 2 hours, until petals curl.

APPLE TURNOVERS

Purchase sufficient number of individual apple turnovers from your local bakery or in the frozen food section of your local grocery. Bake according to directions. Cool, wrap in plastic wrap, serve cold.

This is less of a recipe than a really good idea. Also works well with cherry, blueberry, chocolate, you name it. Enjoy the game!

frozen apple turnovers

FURTHER FEASTINGS

The following selected food and wine events are among those held in Southern California. To obtain a complimentary copy of *California Celebrations*, contact the California Division of Tourism, P.O. Box 1499, Sacramento 95812. To receive information regarding special events held in each community, write or call the city chamber of commerce and/or visitor centers.

January

TET Festival (Huntington Beach) 714-895-8211. Food, entertainment, children's activities.

February

International Food & Music Festival (Camarillo) 805-482-1996. Food, tastings, entertainment.

Taste of Huntington Beach (Huntington Beach) 800-SAY-OCEAN or 714-960-8836. Food, tastings, entertainment.

March

Beans and Jeans Jamboree (Cambria) 800-634-1414 or 805-541-8000; fax 805-543-9498. Food, tastings, cook-off, western dancing.

April

Avocado Festival (Fallbrook) 619-728-5845; fax 619-728-4031. Food, entertainment, contests.

May

Cajun Creole Music Festival (Simi Valley) 805-526-3900. Food, parade, entertainment, arts and crafts, children's activities.

Chili Cook-Off (Apple Valley) 619-247-3521. Food, contests.

Chinese Festival (Santa Barbara) 805-683-3571. Food, entertainment, arts and crafts.

Cinco de Mayo Celebration (Borrego Springs) 619-767-5555; fax 619-767-5976. Food, entertainment, arts and crafts.

Cinco de Mayo Celebration (Calexico) 619-357-1166; fax 619-357-9043. Food, entertainment.

Cinco de Mayo Fiesta (Delano) 805-725-8500. Food, entertainment, fireworks.

Cinco de Mayo Celebration (Oceanside) 619-722-1534. Food, entertainment.

Cinco de Mayo Festival (Santa Maria) 800-549-0036 or 805-922-8824; fax 805-922-4135. Food, entertainment, children's activities.

Jewish Festival (Santa Barbara) 805-963-0244. Food, entertainment, arts and crafts.

Orange Festival (Fillmore) 805-524-5649. Food, entertainment, arts and crafts, parade, train rides.

Pacific Islander Festival (Wilmington) 213-485-2437 or 714-968-1785. Food, entertainment, arts and crafts.

Paso Robles Wine Festival (Paso Robles) 805-239-8463. Food, wine tastings, entertainment.

Strawberry Festival (Garden Grove) 714-638-0981. Food, entertainment, children's activities.

June

Cajun & Zydeco Festival (Long Beach) 562-427-3713 or 415-386-8677. Food, parade, entertainment, arts and crafts, children's activities.

Cajun Festival (Santa Barbara) 805-969-6606. Food, entertainment, arts and crafts.

Irish Festival (Santa Barbara) 805-969-0571. Food, entertainment, arts and crafts.

Morro Bay Salmon Fest (Morro Bay) 800-231-0592 or 805-772-4467. Food, entertainment.

Peddler's Fair & Gourmet Food Tasting (San Juan Bautista) 408-623-2454. Food, tastings, arts and crafts.

July

Greek Festival (Santa Barbara) 805-683-4492. Food, entertainment.

Indian Gathering (Ahwahnee) 209-683-3631. Food, entertainment, arts and crafts.

Obon Festival (San Jose) 408-293-9292. Food, entertainment, games.

Obon Festival (Santa Maria) 800-549-0036 or 805-925-8824; fax 805-922-4135. Food, entertainment, games.

Redlands Chili Cook-Off and Fire Muster (Redlands) 909-793-2546. Food.

Rotary Barbecue and Fireworks (Big Bear Lake) 909-866-8959. Food, entertainment, fireworks.

Sespe Creek Chili Cook-Off and Car Show (Fillmore) 805-524-5649; fax 805-524-2551. Food, entertainment, arts and crafts, train rides, fireworks.

Taste of Camarillo Wine & Food Tasting & Wine Auction (Camarillo) 805-482-8113. Food, tastings, auction.

August

Central Coast Wine Festival (San Luis Obispo) 800-549-3153 or 805-541-1721; fax 805-781-3165. Food, tastings.

Festa Italiana (Santa Barbara) 805-687-7197. Food, entertainment, arts and crafts.

Gourmet Food and Wine Tasting Festival (Torrance) 310-540-5858. Food, entertainment, silent auction.

Monterey Bay Rib Cook-Off (Seaside) 408-394-6501; fax 408-394-1977. Food, entertainment, arts and crafts, farmers' market.

Monterey Winemakers Celebration (Monterey) 408-375-9400; fax 408-655-0354. Food, wine tasting, entertainment.

Nisei Week Japanese Festival (Los Angeles) 213-687-7193; fax 213-687-6510. Food, parade, entertainment, children's activities.

Old Spanish Days Fiesta (Santa Barbara) 805-962-8101. Food, parade, entertainment, arts and crafts, children's activities, rodeo.

Plum Peachy Festival (Loomis) 916-652-7251. Food, entertainment, arts and crafts, farmers' market.

Powwow (Costa Mesa) 714-530-0221. Food, entertainment, arts and crafts.

Salsa Festival (Oxnard) 805-385-7545. Food, tastings, entertainment, arts and crafts.

Taste in San Pedro (San Pedro) 310-832-7272; fax 310-832-0685. Food, entertainment.

September

Grape Bowl Festival (Sanger) 209-857-4575; fax 209-875-0745. Food, entertainment, children's activities.

La Fiesta de San Gabriel (San Gabriel) 818-457-3035 x229. Food, entertainment, children's activities, Blessing of the Animals.

Mexican Independence Day Celebration (Santa Maria) 800-549-0036 or 805-925-824; fax 805-922-4135. Food, entertainment.

Newport Seafest (Newport Beach) 714-729-4400; fax 714-729-4417. Food, entertainment, arts and crafts, games, boat show.

Oktoberfest (Huntington Beach) 714-895-8020; fax 714-895-6011. Food, brew, entertainment.

Oktoberfest (Torrance) 310-327-4384; fax 310-327-6560. Food, entertainment, games, yodeling.

Raisin Festival (Dinuba) 209-591-2707. Food, parade, entertainment, arts and crafts.

October

Harvest Hoedown Festival (Fallbrook) 619-728-4031. Food, entertainment, contests.

Harvest Wine Fair and Country Harvest Tour (Paso Robles) 805-238-0506; fax 805-238-0527. Food, wine tasting, seminars.

Maturango Junction Chili Cook-Off (Ridgecrest) 619-375-6900; fax 619-375-0479. Food, entertainment.

Mountain Apple Fest Arts and Crafts Fair (Bass Lake) 209-642-3676. Food, entertainment, arts and crafts, contests.

Oktoberfest (Bakersfield) 805-327-2424; fax 805-327-2921. Food, brew, entertainment, silent auction.

Oktoberfest (Carlsbad) 619-434-6093. Food, entertainment.

Oktoberfest (Huntington Beach) 714-895-8020; fax 714-895-6011. Food, brew, entertainment.

Octoberfest (Santa Barbara) 805-967-6422. Food, entertainment, arts and crafts.

Pumpkin Festival (Calabasas) 818-222-5680. Food, entertainment, arts and crafts, contest.

Springville Apple Festival (Springville) 209-539-2312. Food, entertainment, arts and crafts, 5K and 10K runs.

December

Christmas on the Prado (San Diego) 619-239-2001; fax 619-339-2749. Food, entertainment, arts and crafts, Santa Lucia Procession.

Christmas Parade & Bazaar (Fillmore) 805-524-5649; fax 805-524-2551. Food, parade, entertainment, arts and crafts.

Winterfest (Lake Elsinore) 909-674-3124; fax 909-674-2392. Food, parade, entertainment, arts and crafts, horse-drawn carriage rides.

SOUTHERN CALIFORNIA: CERTIFIED FARMERS' MARKETS

California's agriculture is recognized as among the finest in the world. There's nothing quite like fresh-picked produce, field-grown flowers, and warm-from-the-oven baked goods. All these, and more, are available at local farmers' markets held in most counties and communities around the state.

These selected farmers' markets are held in festival cities and counties included in this book. For additional information regarding these and other farmers' markets, contact area chambers of commerce and/or visitor centers.

Arroyo Grande

Branch & Mason, Saturday, 11:45 A.M. to 3:30 P.M., 805-544-9570.

Oak Park & Highway 101, Wednesday, 9 A.M. to 11:30 A.M., 805-544-9570.

Atascadero

West Mall & El Camino Real, Wednesday, 3 P.M. to dark, 805-238-5634.

Buellton

Avenue of the Flags & Highway 246, Sunday, 10 A.M. to 2 P.M., 805-688-5736.

Carpinteria

Linden Avenue, Thursday, 4 P.M. to 7 P.M., 805-962-5354.

Coronado

1st & B, Tuesday, 2:30 P.M. to 6 P.M., 619-424-4416.

Fresno County

Clovis/Pollasky between 4th & 5th, Friday, 5 P.M. to 9 P.M. (May-September), 209-298-5774.

Coalinga/Coalinga Plaza, Tuesday, 6 P.M. to 9 P.M., (May-September), 209-935-2948.

Goleta

Calle Real Shopping Center, Thursday, 3 P.M. to 7 P.M., 805-962-5354.

Kern County

Bakersfield/Gottschalk's Court, Sunday, 1 P.M. to 5 P.M.; Tuesday, 3 P.M. to 6 P.M., 805-324-1863.

Bakersfield/30th & F, Saturday, 8 A.M. to 11 A.M., no phone.

Bakersfield/Outback Steakhouse, Thursday, 3 P.M. to 6 P.M.; Saturday, 2 P.M. to 5 P.M., no phone.

Bakersfield/Mt. Vernon & University, Tuesday, 2 P.M. to 5:30 P.M.; Friday, 2 P.M. to 5:30 P.M., 805-873-0477.

Bakersfield/Brimhall & Coffee, Saturday, 9 A.M. to 1 P.M., 805-873-0477.

Kern City/Kern City Center, Thursday, 2 P.M. to 5:30 P.M., 805-873-0477.

Kingsburg

Tulare & 18th, Thursday, 5 P.M. to 7:30 P.M. (July-September), 209-897-2933.

Long Beach

51st & Long Beach Blvd., Saturday, 7:30 A.M. to 11:30 A.M., 562-433-3881.

Downtown/3rd & Broadway, Friday 10 A.M. to 4 P.M., 562-433-3881.

Los Angeles/Hollywood

Los Angeles/2936 West 8th, Monday, 1:30 P.M. to 4:30 P.M., 818-954-9668

Los Angeles/Adams & Vermont, Wednesday, 2 P.M. to 6 P.M., 213-777-1755.

Los Angeles/Wilshire & West Lake, Sunday, 8 A.M. to 1 P.M., 213-385-7800.

Hollywood/Ivar & Hollywood, Sunday, 8:30 A.M. to 1 P.M., 213-463-3171.

Monterey

980 Fremont, Thursday, 2:30 P.M. to 6 P.M., 408-728-5060.

Old Monterey Marketplace, Tuesday, 4 P.M. to 8 P.M., 408-665-8070.

Morro Bay

2650 North Main, Thursday, 3 P.M. to 5 P.M., 805-544-9570

1275 Embarcadero, Friday, 6 P.M. to 9 P.M., 805-772-4467

Ojai

300 East Matilija, Sunday, 10 A.M. to 2 P.M., 805-646-4444.

Oxnard

Plaza Park, 5th & B, Thursday, 10 A.M. to 1 P.M., 805-483-7960.

Channel Islands Harbor, 2810 South Harbor Blvd., Sunday, 10 A.M. to 2 P.M., 805-985-4852.

Esplanade Mall, Highway 101 & Vineyard, Monday, 2:30 P.M. to 6:30 P.M., 805-529-6266.

Pasadena

Victory Park, Saturday, 8:30 A.M. to 1 P.M., 818-449-0179.

Villa Park Community Center, Tuesday, 9:30 A.M. to 1:30 P.M., 818-449-0179.

Paso Robles

14th & Spring, Tuesday, 9:30 A.M. to 12:30 P.M., 805-238-5634.

12th & Spring, Friday, 4 P.M. to 8 P.M., 805-238-5634.

Pismo Beach

Main & Dolliver, Tuesday, 4 P.M. to 8 P.M. (May-October), 805-544-9570.

Redondo Beach

Redondo Beach Pier, Thursday, 9 A.M. to 1 P.M., 310-540-0722.

Reedley

Pioneer Park, Friday, 4:30 P.M. to 7:30 P.M. (May-August), 209-638-5484.

Riverside

Riverside/Arlington, Friday, 8:30 A.M. to noon, 619-244-2772.

Riverside County

La Quinta/Calle Estado & Bermuda, Friday, 6 P.M. to 9 P.M., (6 times a year), 619-564-3199.

Moreno Valley/Moreno Valley Mall, Friday, 5 P.M. to 8 P.M., 619-244-2772.

Palm Springs Village Fest/Palm Canyon Drive & Amado, Thursday, 6 P.M. to 9 P.M., 760-320-3781.

Palm Springs Market Faire/Ramon & Crossley, Friday & Sunday, 8 A.M. to 3 P.M., 760-327-1109.

San Bernardino County

Redlands/East State & Orange, Thursday, 6 P.M. to 9:30 P.M., 909-798-7548.

San Luis Obispo

Gottschalk parking lot, Saturday, 8 A.M. to 10:30 A.M., 805-544-9570.

Higuera Street, Thursday, 6:30 P.M. to 9 P.M., 805-544-9570.

San Luis Obispo County

Baywood/Los Osos, Monday, 2 P.M. to 5 P.M., 805-238-5634.

Cambria/Veterans' Memorial Hall, Friday, 2:30 P.M. to 5:30 P.M., 805-927-4715.

Morro Bay/2650 North Main, Thursday, 3 P.M. to 5 P.M., 805-544-9570.

Morro Bay/1275 Embarcadero parking lot, Friday, 6 P.M. to 9 P.M., 805-772-4467.

Oceano/Oceano Memorial Park, Friday, 2 P.M. to 7 P.M. (April-November), 805-473-2830.

Santa Barbara

500-600 blocks State Street, Tuesday, 4 P.M. to 7:30 P.M., 805-962-5354.

Coast Village Road, Friday, 8:30 A.M. to noon, 805-962-5354.

Santa Barbara & Cota, Saturday, 8:30 A.M. to 12:30 P.M., 805-962-5354.

Santa Barbara County

Guadalupe/9th & Guadalupe, Sunday, 11 A.M. to 3 P.M. (July-November) 805-473-4877.

Lompoc/Ocean & I, Friday, 2 P.M. to 6 P.M., 805-343-2135.

Montecito/1200 Coast Village, Friday, 8:30 A.M. to 12:30 P.M., 805-962-5354.

Orcutt/Bradley & Clark, Tuesday, 10 A.M. to 1 P.M., 805-343-2135.

Temecula

Old Town Plaza, Thursday, 2 P.M. to 5 P.M., 909-699-8138.

Thousand Oaks

Village Square Center, Thursday, 4 P.M. to 7 P.M. 805-529-6266.

Ventura

Main & Mills, Wednesday, 10 A.M. to 1 P.M., 805-529-6266.

Main Street & California, Thursday, 5:30 P.M. to 9:00 P.M., 805-529-6266.

Ventura State Beach, Friday, 9:30 A.M. to 1:30 P.M., 805-529-6266

Victorville

Victor Valley College, Thursday, 8 A.M. to noon, 619-247-3769.

INFORMATION DIRECTORY

For information and details regarding special events, restaurants, lodging, shopping, and attractions contact the following:

Apple Blossom Festival (Oak Glen)

Oak Glen Applegrowers Association, P.O. Box 1123, Oak Glen 92399, 909-790-9470.

Yucaipa Chamber of Commerce, P.O. Box 45, 35145 Yucaipa Boulevard, Yucaipa 92399, 909-790-1841.

Apple Days Festival (Julian)

Julian Chamber of Commerce, P.O. Box 413, Julian 92036, 619-765-1857.

Artichoke Festival (Castroville)

Castroville Artichoke Festival, P.O. Box 1041, Castroville 95012, 408-633-2465; fax 408-633-0485.

Castroville Chamber of Commerce, P.O. Box 744, Castroville 95012, 408-633-6545.

Avocado Festival (Carpinteria)

Carpinteria Avocado Festival, P.O. Box 146, Carpinteria 93013, 805-684-0038.

Carpinteria Valley Chamber of Commerce, 5320 Carpinteria Avenue, Suite J, Carpinteria 93014, 805-684-5479.

Balloon & Wine Festival (Temecula Valley)

Temecula Valley Balloon & Wine Festival, 27475 Ynez Road, Suite 335, Temecula 92591, 909-676-4713.

Temecula Valley Chamber of Commerce, 27450 Ynez Road, Suite 104, Temecula 92591, 909-676-5090.

Basil Festival (Paso Robles)

Sycamore Farms, Route 1, Box 49A, Highway 46 West, Paso Robles 93446, 800-576-5288 or 805-238-5288.

Paso Robles Chamber of Commerce Visitor Center, 1225 Park Street, Paso Robles 93446, 800-406-4040 or 805-238-0506.

Blossom Trail (Fresno County)

Fresno County Convention & Visitors Bureau, 808 M Street, Fresno 93721, 800-788-0836 or 209-233-0836; fax 209-445-0122.

Bounty of the County Food & Wine Tour (San Luis Obispo County)

San Luis Obispo County Visitors & Conference Bureau, 1041 Chorro Street, Suite E, San Luis Obispo 93401, 800-634-1414 or 805-541-8000; fax 805-543-1255.

California Mid-State Beerfest (Atascadero)

Atascadero Elks Club, P.O. Box 1085, Atascadero 93423, 805-466-2044.

Atascadero Chamber of Commerce, 6550 El Camino Real, Atascadero 93422, 805-466-2044.

Celebration of Harvest (Santa Barbara County)

Santa Barbara Vintners' Association, P.O. Box 1558, Santa Ynez 93460, 800-218-0881 or 805-688-0881; fax 805-686-6881.

Santa Barbara Conference & Visitors Bureau, 510 State Street, Suite A, Santa Barbara 93101, 800-676-1266 or 805-966-9222; fax 805-966-1728.

Celebration of Herbs (Squaw Valley)

Squaw Valley Herb Garden, 31765 East Kings Canyon Road, Squaw Valley 93675, 209-332-2909.

Celebration of Western Culture (Kern County)

Kern County CattleWomen, P.O. Box 81436, Bakersfield 93380. (no phone)

Kern County Board of Trade, 2101 Oak Street, Bakersfield 93302, 805-861-2017.

Clam Festival (Pismo Beach)

Pismo Beach Chamber of Commerce, 581 Dolliver Street, Pismo Beach 93449, 800-443-7778 or 805-773-4382.

French Festival (Santa Barbara)

French Festival, 805-564-PARIS (24-hour information line).

Santa Barbara Conference & Visitors Bureau, 12 East Carrillo Street, Santa Barbara 93101, 800-922-4688 or 805-966-9222; fax 805-966-1728.

Fresh Fruit Festival (Reedley)

Reedley District Chamber of Commerce & Visitors Bureau, 1613 12th Street, Reedly 93654, 209-638-3548; fax 209-638-8479.

Grapefruit Festival (Borrego Springs)

Borrego Springs Chamber of Commerce, P.O. Box 66, 622 Palm Canyon Drive, Borrego Springs 92004, 619-767-5555; fax 619-767-5976.

Grecian Festival by-the-Sea (Long Beach)

Assumption of the Blessed Virgin Mary, Greek Orthodox Church, 5761 Colorado Street, Long Beach 90814, 562-494-8929 or 562-220-0730.

Long Beach Area Convention & Visitors Bureau, One World Trade Center, Suite 300, Long Beach 90830, 800-4LB-STAY or 310-436-3645; fax 310-435-5653.

Harbor Festivial (Morro Bay)

Morro Bay Harbor Festival, P.O. Box 1869, 895 Napa Avenue, Suite A-3, Morro Bay 93443, 800-366-6043 or 805-772-1155; fax 805-772-2107.

Morro Bay Chamber of Commerce, 895 Napa Avenue, Suite A-1, Morro Bay 93442, 800-231-0592 or 805-772-4467.

Harvest Festival (Arroyo Grande)

Arroyo Grande Chamber of Commerce, 800 West Branch Street, Arroyo Grande 93420, 805-489-1488; fax 805-489-2239.

Hollywood Bowl Summer Festival (Los Angeles/Hollywood)

Hollywood Bowl Summer Festival, 2301 North Highland Avenue, Los Angeles 90078, 213-972-7300; reservations 213-850-2000; fax 213-851-5617.

Los Angeles Visitor Information Center, 685 South Figueroa Street, Los Angeles 90017, 213-689-8822 or Los Angeles Convention & Visitors Bureau, 633 West Fifth Street, Los Angeles 90071, 213-624-7300.

Huck Finn Jubilee (Victorville)

Mojave Narrows Regional Park, P.O. Box 361, 18000 Yates Road, Victorville 92393, 619-245-2226.

Victorville Chamber of Commerce, 14174 Green Tree Boulevard, Victorville 92393, 619-245-6506.

International Tamale Festival (Indio)

Indio Chamber of Commerce, 82-503 Highway 111, Indio 92201, 800-44-INDIO or 619-347-0676; fax 619-347-6069.

Lemon Festival (Goleta)

Goleta Chamber of Commerce, 5730 Hollister Avenue, Suite 1, Goleta 93116, 800-6-GOLETA or 805-967-4618.

Lobster Festival (Redondo Beach)

Redondo Lobster Festival, King Harbor Association, 181 North Harbor Drive, Redondo Beach 90227, 310-374-2171.

Redondo Beach Visitors Bureau, P.O. Box 3057, Redondo Beach 90227, 800-282-0333 or 310-374-2171.

Mexican Fiesta & Mariachi Music Festival (Ojai)

Ojai Valley Mexican Fiesta & Mariachi Music Festival, P.O. Box 242, Ojai 93024, 805-646-4757.

Ojai Valley Chamber of Commerce, 338 East Ojai Avenue, Ojai 93023, 805-646-3000; fax 805-646-9762.

National Date Festival (Indio)

National Date Festival, Fairgrounds Administration Office, 46350 Arabia Street, Indio 92201, 619-863-8247; fax 619-863-8973.

Indio Chamber of Commerce, 82-503 Highway 111, Indio 92201, 800-44-INDIO or 619-347-0676; fax 619-347-6069.

Obon Festival (San Luis Obispo)

San Luis Obispo Buddhist Temple, 6996 Ontario Road, San Luis Obispo 93041, 805-595-2625.

San Luis Obispo Chamber of Commerce, 1039 Chorro Street, San Luis Obispo 93401, 805-781-2777; fax 805-543-1255.

Olivas Adobe Fiesta (Ventura)

Olivas Adobe Fiesta, P.O. Box 99, 4200 Olivas Park Drive, Ventura 93002, 805-648-5823.

Ventura Visitors & Convention Bureau, 89-C South California Street, Ventura 93001, 800-333-2989 or 805-648-2075; fax 805-648-2150.

Orange Blossom Festival (Riverside)

Orange Blossom Festival, P.O. Box 1603, Riverside 92502, 800-382-8202 or 909-715-3400.

Riverside Convention & Visitors Bureau, 3443 Orange Street, Riverside 92501, 909-787-7950.

Pie Festival (Malibu)

Malibu United Methodist Church, 30128 Morning View Drive, Malibu 90265, 310-457-7505.

Malibu Chamber of Commerce, 23805 Stuart Ranch Road, Suite 100, Malibu 90265, 213-456-9025; fax 310-456-0195.

Pitchin', Cookin', & Spittin' Hullabaloo (Calico)

Calico Ghost Town, P.O. Box 638, 36600 Ghost Town Road, Yermo 92398, 800-TO-CALICO or 619-254-2122.

Raisin Festival (Selma)

Selma District Chamber of Commerce, 1802 Tucker Street, Selma 93662, 209-896-3315.

Rededication Celebration (Allensworth)

Colonel Allensworth State Historic Park, Star Route 1, Box 148, Earlimart 93219, 805-849-3433.

Renaissance Pleasure Faire (San Bernardino County)

Renaissance Pleasure Fair, 800-52-FAIRE (event hotline)

San Bernardino Convention & Visitors Bureau, 201 North E Street, Suite 103, San Bernardino 92401, 800-TO-RTE-66 or 909-889-3980; fax 909-888-5998.

Scandinavian Festival (Thousand Oaks)

California Lutheran University, Public Relations Office, 60 West Olsen Road, Thousand Oaks 91360, 805-493-3151.

Conejo Valley Chamber of Commerce, 625 West Hillcrest Drive, Thousand Oaks 91360, 805-499-1993; fax 805-498-7264.

Souper 101 Roundup (Buellton)

Buellton Visitors Information Center, 376 Avenue of the Flags, P.O. Box 231, Buellton 93427, 800-324-3800 or 805-688-STAY; fax 805-688-5399.

Squid Festival (Monterey)

The Great Monterey Squid Festival, 2600 Garden Road, Suite 208, Monterey 93940, 408-649-6547; fax 408-649-4124.

Monterey County Visitors & Convention Bureau, P.O. Box 1770, 380 Alvarado Street, Monterey 93942, 408-649-1770; fax 408-649-3502.

Strawberry Festival (Oxnard)
Greater Oxnard & Harbors Tourism Bureau, 200 West Seventh Street, Oxnard 93030, 800-2-OXNARD or 805-385-7545; fax 805-385-7571.

Strawberry Festival (Santa Maria)
Santa Maria Valley Chamber of Commerce/Visitor & Convention Bureau, 614 South Broadway, Santa Maria 93454, 800-331-3779 or 805-925-2403.

Summer Farmers Market (Coronado)
Coronado Bay Resort, 4000 Coronado Bay Road, Coronado 92118, 619-424-4000.

Coronado Visitor Information, 111 Orange Avenue, Suite A, Coronado 92118, 800-622-8300 or 619-437-8788; fax 619-437-6006.

Swedish Festival (Kingsburg)
California Welcome Center, P.O. Box 515, 1776 Sixth Avenue Drive, Kingsburg 93631, 209-897-2925; fax 209-897-4621.

Taste of Solvang (Solvang)
Solvang Conference & Visitors Bureau, P.O. Box 70, Solvang 93464, 800-468-6765 or 805-688-6144; fax 805-688-8620.

Taste of Ventura County (Ventura County)
Channel Islands Harbor Visitor Center, 3810 West Channel Islands Boulevard, Suite G, Oxnard 93035, 800-994-4852 or 805-985-4852; fax 805-985-7952.

Tournament of Roses/Rose Bowl Game (Pasadena)
Pasadena Convention & Visitors Bureau, 171 South Los Robles Avenue, Pasadena 91101, 818-795-9311; fax 818-795-9656.

INDEX

O

P

Q

R

S

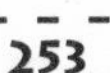

ABOUT THE AUTHOR

Bob Carter is an award-winning travel writer and columnist. He has served on the faculty of Pasadena City College; California State University, Los Angeles; and the University of Oregon. He received a 1993 "Best of Series of Short Stories" award from the Outdoor Writers Association of California. He is an active member of the International Food, Wine, & Travel Writers Association and Outdoor Writers Association of California. His ongoing travel columns appear in a variety of newpapers and magazines. He is author of the popular travel book, *The Best of Central California: Main Roads & Side Trips.* When not traveling, he resides in the coastal community of Oxnard, California.